Much Laughter, A Few Tears

**Memoirs of
a Woman's Friendship
with Betty MacDonald
and Her Family**

by Blanche Caffiere

Order this book online at www.trafford.com
or email orders@trafford.com

Most Trafford titles are also available at major online book retailers.

© Copyright 2005, 2011 Blanche Caffiere.
Original copyright 1992

Note for Librarians: A cataloguing record for this book is available from Library and Archives Canada at www.collectionscanada.ca/amicus/index-e.html

Printed in the United States of America.

ISBN: 978-1-4269-6608-8 (sc)

Trafford rev. 04/14/2011

 www.trafford.com

North America & international
toll-free: 1 888 232 4444 (USA & Canada)
phone: 250 383 6864 ♦ fax: 812 355 4082

Table of Contents

PART 3

PART 4

Acknowledgements

$\mathcal{T}$o my husband, Cyril, who proofread and put up with the constant typing and lack of cooking; to my granddaughter, Katy von Brandenfels, who proofread and suggested; to Al Riddle, whose computer knowledge saw me through little crises; to Alison Bard Barnett, who read and authenticated the manuscript—and laughed a lot; to Garland Norin, my mentor and advisor; to Joyce Delbridge and the memoir group for making positive suggestions; to Alison Swaisland, who came all the way from Rome, Italy, to find Betty MacDonald's house and urged me to write about our friendship; to Bridget Culligan for her artistic contributions; to Deborah Kaufmann, whose professional expertise was invaluable; and to my ninety-seven year old friend and neighbor, Helen Clancy, who asked almost every day, "When are you going to write that book?" I thank them all.

Betty MacDonald at the peak of her success in 1946.

*Dedicated to all the
Betty MacDonald Fans*

Preface

As an early adolescent I recognized that the Bards, Betty MacDonald's family, were special. All through high school I considered an invitation to the Bards' house an assurance of a good time. Then, after graduation, our paths took different directions. Betty went to the University of Washington while I attended teachers' college in Bellingham, Washington. Her next step was marriage and becoming the mother of two girls while mine was teaching in a rural school in the Nooksack Valley near Mt. Baker.

Then Betty returned to her mother's home in the University District while I taught in Federal Way near Seattle. It was my fortune to have our paths cross again at this juncture, only to change again when I married, gave birth to a daughter, and moved to Portland. I spent a number of years there, meeting new friends and having new experiences, but I always missed my contacts with the Bard family.

Betty and I were destined to have our paths cross again. This time it was on Vashon Island. Neither of us knew the other was moving there, but when we found out, our relationship picked up right where it had left off. Riding the ferries between Seattle and Vashon or walking down the streets of the little town, it was as though someone had struck a match and lit two candles. We were immediately turned on. While living on the island, our friendship blossomed full blown. We teased each other, entertained each other, and laughed long and often.

Toward the last part of our lives there, Betty became famous. She was being feted all over the United States while I returned to Portland after World War II, where I eventually was divorced.

Betty moved to Carmel Valley and I returned to Seattle to be near my family. Not long after my move, Betty returned to Seattle also, but her health was poor, and she was not to live very much longer. Thus our paths crossed again for the fourth and last time.

Through all the years I have entertained my friends by telling them stories about the Bards. At the urging of these friends I have finally written them down—stories of when Betty, her family and I were on the same path, plus a few tales of the "in-between" times.

PART

1

CHAPTER 1

An Evening at the Bards'

*B*etsy's hand was always waving in the air in Miss Taggart's Latin class at Lincoln High School in Seattle in 1920. Betsy and I were freshmen, and she sat across the room from me. I was fascinated with her from the very first day of school. She had reddish-brown hair, hazel eyes, and braces on her teeth. These were the first braces I had ever seen. Betsy also wore a round comb in her hair, which she kept manipulating in between raising her hand. Frequently she wore a blue chambray dress, Norfolk style, with a black patent leather belt laced through the panels. She confided in me that it was her uniform from St. Nicholas School, which she and her older sister had attended in previous years. When her father died suddenly, her mother thought public school would be more practical than the expensive, private one.

I was happy when we were assigned lockers next to each other as that gave us a chance to have short visits. One day as we were putting our books away, a girl we both knew slightly who had pale blue eyes, disheveled brown hair, and wore wire-rimmed glasses, stopped by and made a remark. It was not meant to be funny, but her appearance plus the remark tickled us both and we could scarcely wait for her to pass by before we burst into giggles. Betsy said, "You know, don't you, that she combs her hair with an egg beater?" At that moment we discovered that we laughed at exactly the same kinds of things.

In our short visits, I learned piecemeal that Betsy's mother had invited Miss Taggert to dinner, and that they were on such friendly terms that Miss Taggert said when they were away from school they could call her by her first name, Eunice. I thought Miss Taggert was one of those superhuman beings and was completely awed that she was a personal friend of Betsy's family.

"Speaking of names," Betsy said, "my real name is Ann Elizabeth Campbell Bard; Betsy is a nickname." (When Betsy entered college, she changed her name to Betty as she thought it sounded more sophisticated. Later she told me she wished she hadn't.) I had never known a girl before who not only had braces on her teeth and a round comb, but invited a teacher for dinner and had such a long name as well. I knew I was making a new, special friend.

We arranged to have lunch together the next day — sack lunches brought from home. At lunch time we visited about our respective families until the bell rang and we had to run to class. Betty told me she had an older sister, Mary, a younger brother, Cleve, and two little sisters, Dede and Alison.

I told her about my brothers, thirteen and nine years older than I, and my sister, eleven years older. I added that one brother had a knack for getting into trouble. Immediately she picked up on that and wanted to know what kind of trouble. I usually didn't tell my friends about Ralph's escapades, but I sensed that Betsy would enjoy hearing about some of them. So I told her how he had thrown several boys' caps on top of the school building and they had to call the fire department to get them down, and how he had thrown a snowball at a teacher and hit her in the heel. Betsy listened so eagerly and asked so many questions, I got the impression that I was much more entertaining with a brother like Ralph to tell about than I was before. As we raced to our class, she said, "Mother would love to hear your stories. Can't you come home with me? How about tonight?"

Immediately after school we got to a phone, and after her mother said it would be very nice if I came home with her, I phoned my mother, fully confident she would let me, as she was very permissive as long as things were moral. Often she told me that the angel of the wild things was watching over me, and I totally believed her.

I was thrilled to be going home with a new school friend, especially since the friend was so unusual in so many ways. Instead of going north to the Green Lake streetcar, we headed east and took the Wallingford car, transferring to the Laurelhurst bus at Forty-fifth and University Way. There were only Laurelhurst school kids on this bus. Then, as now, Laurelhurst was a posh place to live, and I felt socially upgraded traveling with this noisy bunch.

The bus wound around the Laurelhurst hills, delivering each youngster until it reached the end of the line: the Palisades.

Here there were no paved streets, only open fields and knobby fruit trees with a cow grazing underneath, tied to a stake. On a little knoll stood Betsy's house, white Victorian. As we entered the front door, Betsy's mother, Mrs. Bard — or Sydney, as she asked both young and old to call her — met us. She was tall and thin, with patrician features, smartly plain in dress, and extremely warm and charming.

We dropped our schoolbooks in a chair and went directly to the big country kitchen where Gammy, Betsy's grandmother, reigned as queen. She was wearing a white apron with a limp bottom ruffle and a little white boudoir cap. (Many women in the twenties wore these caps in order to avoid combing their long hair the minute they arose from bed in the morning.) The door to her small bedroom was open, and there was the rumpled bed with her treasures strewn about, just as Betty later describes in her book, *The Egg and I*. Gammy helped Betsy with a snack and then we walked through the large dining room. I was enchanted to see an enormous oval dining table partially set with Halloween favors at each place: jack-o'-lanterns, witches on broomsticks, owls, and black cats. Betsy told me they had been delivered from Augustine and Kyers, a famous grocery store located at First and Cherry in downtown Seattle. Augustine and Kyers delivered all over town — if you paid their prices. Their reputation in Seattle was similar to Harrod's in London or Bloomingdale's in New York. Was my visit special enough for her to have ordered these favors?

When we ate, Sydney sat at the head of the table. In front of her were beautiful Wedgewood platters filled with fried chicken, mashed potatoes and gravy. She served, wielding her ornate carving set effectively. Mary arrived a little late with an unexpected guest, but another place was set with no ado. Gammy ate in the kitchen on the breadboard because, she claimed, it was more peaceful. There was much talking and laughing at the table, but soon Betsy interrupted everyone. "Now, Blanche, tell your story about your brother, Ralph, throwing all the kids' caps up on the roof of the schoolhouse, and how the fire department had to be called to come and get them." I felt a sense of inadequacy as I repeated the tale, but struggled through, hoping it would measure up to Sydney's expectations.

Immediately after dinner, some boys came to pick up Mary and her friend. Betsy and I were overwhelmed by Mary's popularity. Betsy, anxious to be the genial hostess all the way, invited me upstairs to see her big sister's formals. She pulled open the sliding doors of the closet and there was an array of long party dresses in as many colors as you would find on a color wheel. Betsy took a pink one off the hanger, held it out to me, and said, "Try it on."

I had never worn a formal before so I quickly slipped out of my navy blue school clothes and slithered into this shimmering satin gown. Betsy chose a yellow one, and we preened in front of the full-length mirror, our heavy school shoes poking out underneath. Caught up in this party mood, Betsy said, "I'll phone Ted Sutton. His dad lets him drive their car, and he can bring Bunny Redman along." I stood in utter amazement while these plans materialized. Betty was arranging real dates for us! I had never had a real date, and to go on one dressed in a pink formal was the ultimate.

In a few minutes a big Franklin car stopped in front, and after the boys said hello to Sydney, they ushered us into the back seat of the car while they sat in front and talked about the various items on the dashboard. They were completely oblivious to our gorgeous gowns under our school coats.

Ted said, "We can go anywhere as the gas tank is full, but I have to be home at eight o'clock." We headed for the University District and drove up and down the "Ave" while we gazed superiorly at the poor people who had to walk. Since neither our family nor anyone else we knew owned a car, just to get into one was pretty new to me. Betsy suggested that we drive to Willard's Roadhouse, which was a few miles north of the city limits and the popular place to go for dinner dancing. All Ted did was cruise into the Roadhouse's circular driveway, swing around the garden of shrubs and drive back out to the main highway. But technically, we had been there. I could visualize myself telling the Green Lake kids of our trip to Willard's, and of all times, on a school night.

We were back at the Bards by eight o'clock and played cards until bedtime. At about ten o'clock, we climbed into the ivory-painted twin beds, but had scarcely settled down when Mary came bursting in. "Guess what, Betsy? Ray kissed me good night!" Mary was bright-eyed and glowing, her copper-colored hair falling to her shoulders. I was half-shocked and yet admired her openness. I thought a kiss was something you didn't breathe the likes of which to a soul.

Betsy became so exhilarated over the progress of Mary's

romance that she said, "I'm not one bit sleepy, are you? Let's go down to the kitchen and make a batch of fudge."

There were no limits to the entertainment my hostess was providing: formals, boys, a car, a roadhouse — and now fudge. At our house you made fudge only on Saturday nights, and nothing went on after the hour of ten because Dad had to get his rest. We were rattling pans, opening a big burlap sack of sugar, and getting milk out of the icebox when Gammy came in dressed in her nightie. I thought she had come to complain, but no, she had come to help.

The fudge was so good, we took the pan upstairs to eat in bed. Finally, saturated in sweets, we turned over and went to sleep. After a few hours of rest, Betsy shook my shoulder. "We have to get up right now or we'll miss the school bus!" We hurried into our clothes and ran down the stairs to the kitchen where Betsy quickly made us toast. Picking up our untouched schoolbooks, we flew out the front door and down the path to the bus, which was waiting for us. Although Betsy lived at the end of the line, there were three kids already on it. The driver said good morning to both of us and we were on our way. When we were well-settled into our seats, I timidly asked, "What about our homework?"

"Oh, we'll get to that right now," Betsy answered lightly as she opened her algebra book. For a fleeting moment I longed for our golden oak dining table with its green-shaded lamp.

I headed the algebra paper as the teacher had taught us and started on the assignment. Concentration was difficult but we began comparing answers, and somehow by the time we had to transfer to the streetcar, we were finished. What a relief! As we settled ourselves on the wooden seats of the Wallingford car, we started on our Latin assignment. I always wrote my translations in a notebook, but Betsy said, "Oh, don't bother with that. We can keep it in our heads. You can raise your hand a lot for the stuff you know, and then you won't get called on for what you don't know." Now I knew why her hand was raised so much at the beginning of every period. I was discombobulated all day, but later, the ride home on the Green Lake streetcar with my regular friends made it all worthwhile. I regaled them with the events of the previous night and they responded by giving me their undivided attention. I felt like a misplaced star from Hollywood.

CHAPTER 2

Waffles at Midnight

$\mathcal{A}$ll the high school kids were outside on the lawns and porches, reluctant to return to their classrooms because it was the first hot day in late spring. The bell had rung, and as I walked toward the door, I saw Betsy coming across the lawn. "Betsy, this is swimmin' weather," I yelled.

"You bet it is," she hollered back. "And I'm going in the minute I get home. Want to come along?"

After a quick phone call to Mother to let her know what was up, Betsy and I met at the north entrance after school, ready to set off for Laurelhurst.

Sydney, her usual cordial self, had a plate of peanut butter sandwiches waiting for us. I had to borrow a bathing suit, and as we walked to the beach, I knew I was going to have difficulty staying in it as it was two sizes too big for me. *But who cares*, I thought, *at last I am going to swim at the famous Palisades on Lake Washington*. My brother had swum there many times and had told me how much better the water was than the algae-ridden waters of Green Lake.

The Bards' house sat back from the lake about a block and we had to walk through a lot of brush to reach the water's edge. Even so, in those days most of the twenty-mile-long lake shore was readily accessible to anyone who wanted to take a dip. (Nowadays I doubt whether you could find a six-foot stretch of Lake Washington shore that isn't covered with a rolling green lawn, a dock jutting into the lake, and a half-million dollar home in the background.)

Betsy and I were the only ones in the water at first, but gradually other swimmers appeared and soon there were over twenty kids swimming about. It was a wonderful climax to a hot school day — so good, that on the walk back to the house we decided to go in after dark as well.

After one of Sydney's tasteful and beautifully served dinners, Caroline Benham and Lucy Nugent, old grammar school friends of Betsy's, dropped by. Caroline dangled a turquoise bathing suit in the air and asked, "Are you in the mood for a moonlight swim?"

With the course of events turning out as they did, perhaps it was fortunate that there was no moonlight that night. When it grew dark enough, the four of us walked to the beach in our clothes, as Betsy advised that it would be too cold to walk back in wet suits. Each of us chose a bush on which to hang our clothes. Caroline and Lucy slid quickly into their bone-dry suits, but Betsy and I were not about to hurry into our soggy ones. "Ooh, Betsy," I said, "my suit feels awful — it is still wet."

"Mine, too," said Betsy. "I hate to pull it up over my stomach. On second thought I don't think I will. Nude swimming is better anyway."

Those days you accepted the fact without the lift of an eyebrow that guys could swim in the nude, but girls…*well, when in Rome, do as the Romans,* I rationalized, quickly dropping my wet suit onto the sand. Caroline turned around and said, "Well, we're not going to miss out on the fun." Lucy threw her suit in the air. "Freedom at last!"

Four naked bodies ran wildly into the water. Oh, the utter luxury of gliding through the soft water, completely unhampered by slipping shoulder straps. We splashed each other, squealed, swam between each other's legs, and stood on our hands while we pushed our legs above the water line, making them look like thin piling.

Suddenly there was the sound of a motor and headlights were glaring at us. "Betsy, what shall we do?" Caroline asked breathlessly. "How will we ever find our clothes, or even get out of the water?" gasped Lucy.

"I don't remember where my personal bush is with all my stuff!" I added my gripe to the others.

"Just stay under the water," Betsy said quietly, "and I'll handle this. I think it's the Smith twins. They are harmless." The driver got out of the car and started toward the lake. "That you, Bruce?" Betsy yelled.

"Yeah, that you, Betsy? How's the water?" Bruce shouted back.

"It's neat. Why don't you kids go home and put your suits on and join us?"

After a quick conference with his brother, Bruce called, "We'll be back in fifteen minutes."

What a relief, Betsy's finesse had worked! "You know," remarked Caroline, "they could have had their suits on, and then what could we have done?"

As soon as Bruce turned the car around, we raced out of the lake, each of us hell-bent on finding her respective bush. I got the wrong one at first and tried to fasten Lucy Nugent's tiny bra around my developing bosom. Betsy could find but one of her shoes. It was quite a struggle to pull underclothes over wet bodies, especially since no one had thought to bring a towel. Finally, with shoes full of sand and twisted clothes, we started up the road when Bruce drove up beside us. "Hey, youse guys, you didn't wait for us."

"Sorry, Bruce," said Betsy, "but we got too cold to wait." And she allowed her teeth to chatter in order to stress the point.

Sydney met us at the door, where we stood with teeth chattering and wet hair dripping onto our shoulders — and her floor. But she didn't mind. "All of you have lavender lips, you're so cold, but come on into the kitchen and lap your lips over these mugs of hot chocolate."

Each mug had a big plump marshmallow floating on top.

Sydney had made this cocoa from scratch in a big stew kettle. It was the kind of cocoa you made from a little paste of chocolate, water and sugar, and then slowly added milk as you stirred and stirred.

"This is the best chocolate I have ever had in my whole life," Lucy declared.

"Sydney, you are saving my life with this hot drink, I've never been so co-o-ld." Caroline was still shivering.

Sydney was further motivated by such appreciative remarks. "How would you girls like some waffles? I have a new electric waffle iron!"

"An electric waffle iron?" I asked. I had never seen any kind but the iron one like ours that we heated on the kitchen range. In no time we were sitting down to tender, golden waffles drowning in maple syrup and butter. The enticing smell brought other members of the family to the table, and before long Betsy's two little sisters came in, dressed in long white nighties with their little pink toes peeking out from under the bottom ruffle. Dede — whose real name was Darsie, after her father — was about five years old and had round, shiny gray eyes and dark brown hair. I wanted to reach over and pat her smooth ivory skin.

"Dede, would you sing something for my friends — how about 'Stumbling All Around'?" asked Betsy. Dede sang the requested song, getting the words and melody exactly right. She could sing all the current popular songs in a clear, true voice.

"And now, Alty, it's your turn to sing for us," announced Betsy as she hoisted her sister Alison up onto a dining room chair. Alty, a little over two years old, had reddish hair, gorgeous amber-colored eyes, and the same lovely satin skin as Dede's. Alty put her plump little hands together to shape a ball and sang, "Here's a ball for baby, big and soft and round, here is baby's hammer, oh, how he can pound!" As she sang the last two lines she rolled her hands into fists and pounded them one against the other. We all clapped. Betsy gave each of her little sisters a big hug and they toddled back upstairs to bed.

Sydney asked us about our swim. I thought for a minute that Betsy wouldn't tell about our nudity, but when she did, Sydney merely answered, "Of course I thought you would do that — it's so much more fun." Then Betsy, who never failed to promote me and my stories, said, "Now, Mother would love to hear about the swim your mother had years ago at Long Beach, California."

So I began. "First of all, let me tell you how my mother happened to tell her experience to me. Last year about this time when I was only thirteen, I had saved my baby-sitting money — ten cents an hour — for a new wool bathing suit. (Then, wool was the only way to go.) I found this adorable powder blue number. It had a sailor collar with silk stripes and eyelets up the front through which ran a silk cord. There was one drawback, however.

"Mother advised me always to get a suit a bit large so it could be worn for two years. This suit came only in one size and it fit to a T — no room in which to grow. However, no other suit I saw had any appeal. After all, it was my hard-earned money, so I bought it for $8.95. I could hardly wait to appear in it at the Green Lake Bathing Beach. The next day, I slipped into it in one of the dressing booths at the bathhouse. As I made my way down the hall with the blue denim bag into which I had put my clothes, I heard a girl say, 'Isn't that a darling suit?' What a lift to be admired by a complete stranger! When I arrived at the counter, I handed the matron my bag in return for which she gave me a big safety pin that had the number of the peg where the bag was hung. But as she handed it to me, she said, 'My dear, would you mind standing back a little so I can see your suit?'

"Proudly I stepped back, expecting admiration. Instead she tipped her bifocals and squinted her eyes. 'You know, my dear, the city rules say that no bathing suit shall be more than four inches above the knee. Let me measure.' She stepped around the counter, took a tape measure from the pocket of her black sateen apron, placed the one-inch mark at the middle of my kneecap and stretched it up to the bottom of my suit.

"'Uh-huh, just as I thought,' she said, 'it measures four-and-a-half inches.'

"A short line of people had formed behind me waiting to check their clothes, and there I stood: an adulterous woman with no Jesus standing near to ask those without sin to cast the first stone. But there was an off duty lifeguard. The matron turned to him and said, 'Hank, that suit is one-half inch too short.'

" 'Only one-half inch — hell, let her go on in,' he said.

" 'Well dear,' she said, suddenly turning sweet, 'Give your suit a good yank and go on.' At first I thought I wouldn't tell Mom about it since she had wanted me to get a bigger suit, but it was on my mind so I finally told her. She thought for a minute and said, 'Well, times have changed a little bit, child, listen to *my* story.

" 'I was in college and I was about twenty — it must have been about 1890. I was swimming in the ocean at Long Beach, dressed in the customary long bathing suit with long stockings meeting the bottoms of the legs of my suit. The stockings were fastened up very well, I thought, until an unusually big wave rolled up and knocked me off my feet. In the struggle to keep from going completely under, my stockings came off and I couldn't find them. A real gentleman was sitting on the sandy beach and saw my predicament. He went over to a nearby clothesline and took a pair of stockings off the line. I couldn't lose my dignity by coming out to get them, so he rolled up his trousers, took off his shoes and stockings, and waded out to me. I was ever so grateful to him, although believe me, I had a terrible time getting those stockings on, standing waist high in the water. Of course when I put my clothes on, I took the stockings back and hung them on the clothesline. So you see, Blanche, in thirty years girls and women have come a long way in gaining freedom to show their bare legs!'"

When I finished talking, Sydney said, "Those are wonderful stories, Blanche — I wonder what women will be wearing in fifty years!"

"Nothing," said Betsy, "if you judge by tonight!"

CHAPTER 3

Baked Shoes

$\mathcal{I}$ had visited the Bards so many times that finally Mother said, "I don't think you should go there one more time without having Betsy come here." I knew she was right, but our home life seemed so dull and stilted compared to the Bards'. How would I entertain her?

Near us was an empty lot where the neighborhood kids played softball, which is what I did when I got home from school every day. But Betsy had never turned out for sports at Lincoln High, and I had seen the way she held a bat in our gym class when we played ball. It was what the kids called "chopping wood."

Behind our property was a good-sized pond. In elementary school when I brought kids home, we would head for the pond, armed with empty jars to catch frogs and tadpoles. My friend Marge said that what she liked about coming to our house after school was not only hunting tadpoles, but eating navy bean sandwiches with mustard, made with Mother's homemade bread. However, her mother complained that she always came home with wet feet. I knew Betsy was too sophisticated for that form of fun. After all, we were in high school now, and furthermore, she had provided boys with a car when I visited her.

All at once an idea came to me. "You know, Mother, Betsy loves her little sisters so much I bet she would like to go out to Esther's. She told me once I was lucky to be an aunt." Esther was my sister, eleven years older than I, married, with three children all under the age of six. She was a people-lover and her coffee pot was always on, ready for neighbors to drop in at any hour of the day. When I approached Esther about it, she said, "I'm dying to meet Betsy — you can bring her out after school. We'll have dinner and you can stay all night. Jack can drive you to school the next morning." Betsy seemed delighted over the invitation.

On the day we chose, it rained incessantly and we had to walk seventeen blocks from the end of the Phinney car line to North Park. I had walked this route many times, but I knew Betsy was used to the school bus coming to her door. However, the two of us plugged along, carrying our schoolbooks and letting the raindrops run off the ends of our noses. Once at Esther's, we stepped into her cozy kitchen where she had a lively fire going in the kitchen range. We draped our wet clothes near the stove and put our shoes on the open oven door to dry.

Esther had a good dinner planned with wild blackberry pie for dessert. The pie was on the drainboard, a symbol of what was about to come. I helped with the dinner while Betsy took charge of the children. She held the baby, Tom, and told stories to Bill and Jackie. She made up wonderful tales, sensing just what would amuse each age.

No wonder her future *Mrs. Piggle Wiggle* stories were so popular. I always read those stories to View Ridge third graders when I was a school librarian in the Seattle school district. Whether or not Betty meant those stories to be behavior modification messages is unknown, but I watched children smile knowingly when they heard about the "Never-want-to-go-to-bed"ers and "Don't-touch-it's-mine" kids. To me, they were funny little stories that poked fun at the characters about whom they were written. Betty was still dealing with two teenagers when her writing was at its peak and she had experienced those very parent-child relationships. I had been present when her girls were coaxing to stay up and Betty promised them stories, if they hurried on upstairs to bed. I went along one or two times and joined in the fun. The next morning we had to hurry in order to be ready for Esther's husband, Jack, to drive us to school. All went well until Betsy attempted to put on her shoes. The hot oven had baked them until they were stiff and shrunken. We massaged the leather by rubbing and twisting, but nothing changed. Finally Betsy crammed her feet down and said, "Well, my feet are in, but they are folded up like fists." She staggered out to the 1920 Ford touring car, and we settled ourselves in the back seat while Jack snapped the isinglass curtains on the sides. It was still raining. When we arrived at Lincoln High, Betsy hobbled up the stairs and into the school.

When I met her at noon, she said, "My feet unfolded a half-hour ago and my shoes now fit again!" Thus I had entertained Betsy, albeit in a much less sophisticated way than she had hosted me.

CHAPTER 4

The Silver Spray

$\mathcal{L}$incoln High School was becoming crowded and a ne
school was going up just north of the University District.
was to be called Roosevelt after Theodore Roosevelt, an
eventually the athletes were to become known as the Roug
Riders. The enrollment would include students from the are
near the University, Laurelhurst, Ravenna, Fairview, an
Green Lake.

When Betsy and I were juniors, the new high school wa
ready to open. On the first day of school, we discovered w
were in the same botany class. Margaret Tomlinson was th
dedicated spinster teacher. She was extremely intelligent, buil
on roly-poly lines, and had long, black hair which she pile
high on top of her head. I have often thought that Betsy's Mrs
Piggle Wiggle was a replica of Miss Tomlinson, at least in looks

Betsy and I agreed that Miss Tomlinson was about the bes
teacher we ever had. She showed so much enthusiasm abou
her subject matter that it carried over to her students. What sh
taught remained with me for life, although at the time I coul
have cared less about photosynthesis or osmosis.

Miss Tomlinson set up intricate paraphernalia to demon
strate how photosynthesis and osmosis came about. It wa
exciting. Betsy and I were hooked on the subject matter im
mediately, and were good students. But we should never have
sat next to each other. Everything Betsy said struck me funny
and everything I said, she laughed at also.

It was at this time I discovered I had a certain gland in my mouth that, if pushed with my tongue, a little rainbow-shaped spray would shoot out. Even my dentist was at a loss to explain how this happened. Since Betsy was always so appreciative of my talents, she was one of the first people with whom I shared this phenomenon. "Why, Blanche, I've never seen another person in my whole life who could do that!" Just then Alice Grumfield came by and Betsy called to her, "Alice, come here and look what Blanche can do. Have you ever seen anyone so talented?"

I pressed my tongue and out came the spray. Alice sprang back, knitted her eyebrows and said, "That's not a spray, that is just plain spit."

Resenting the fact that my unique performance had been demeaned, I answered, "My mother taught me a long time ago never to spit in public."

And Betsy quickly said, "You're wrong, Alice, that isn't even saliva. It's a silver spray, and only Blanche has been granted this rare privilege." Alice moved on down the hall, unconvinced. We decided she had no imagination.

Early in the first week of school, Miss Tomlinson held forth on how appreciative we should all be for this beautiful new school whose teachers had been screened carefully and were Seattle's best. She then launched into the wonders of this particular classroom with the slate-covered lab tables, the extra room in the back for growing molds and bacteria. She called our attention to the large microscopes sitting on each table. "They are worth seventy-five dollars apiece, and you must handle them very carefully. When you have finished with one, put his little gray flannel cap on to keep out the dust. When you are screwing up and down to focus, be sure you don't screw too far or it will come crashing down on the glass slide."

Even as she spoke there was a loud crash directly in front of my seat. An overgrown lad, with watery blue eyes and an oversized nose that perched over a mouth that hung open most of the time, had been unconsciously turning the screw, and had done the exact thing she had said not to do. He stared blankly at the teacher. Betsy whispered, "He's so stupid, silver spray him!" It took little urging. Quietly, I performed my unique art. Naturally he looked up at the ceiling to see if by chance there was some marvelous device in this ultramodern room that dripped on culprits.

"Do it once more," came the orders from Betsy. I gladly obliged. Again, as Miss Tomlinson scolded him, he looked up. "Don't look up at the ceiling, George, look at me and listen to what I am telling you," Miss Tomlinson said. Betsy and I doubled up in laughter, and Miss Tomlinson thought we were laughing at a serious situation, whereas we should be concerned. Little did she know that we were on her side and had punished the bloke in our own way. She asked us to leave the classroom and not come back until we had stopped giggling. Out in the hall we discussed what we should do to make amends.

"We can't tell her about the silver spray; she'd probably call it spitting," I said. I was feeling a little guilty. "We could come in after school and work."

"Yes," said Betsy, "she wants people to come in and water the plants." We did stay after school and told Miss Tomlinson that we were sorry we had laughed because he looked so dumb. She accepted our apology and was glad to have our help.

Both Betsy and her sister, Mary, were totally unafraid of the principal or the teachers. Everyone admired the way they spoke up when they didn't like decisions. One time I happened to be standing in the hall next to the principal. He was very tall, thin, and stately. His thinning hair and little goatee were pale red. His gold Phi Beta Kappa key dangled on a chain from his pocket watch. I considered him extremely unapproachable. But Mary Bard didn't. It had been snowing for almost two hours and all the pupils thought school should be dismissed because no one in Seattle was ever prepared for snow. It had

Captain: LOUISE BANKS "Peggy"
Port of Entry: Lincoln
Ship: Academic
Cargo: Glee Club 3, 4, Opera 3, 4, Good Cheer
Committee 3
Destination: Music

Captain: BETSY BARD "Bard"
Port of Entry: Lincoln
Ship: Academic
Cargo: Chr. School Improvement Com. 3 Chr.
Good Cheer Com. 4, Senior Dance Com. 4,
Vaudeville Com. 3, Freshman Entertainment 3,
4, Standard Pin Com. 3, Glee Club 3, 4
Destination: To be an illustrator

Captain: BLANCHE HAMILTON "Botch"
Port of Entry: Lincoln
Ship: Academic
Cargo: Improvement Committee 3, Grammar
School Committee 3, Girls' Club Cabinet 4,
Member Rose Garden 3, Honor Society 3, 4,
Chief Clerk "News" 4, Senior Honor Roll,
Girls' Athletics 1, 2, 3, 4
Destination: U. of W.

Betty and Blanche (center) in Roosevelt High School year book, 1924 graduating class.

just been announced that school would not be dismissed. Mary ran up to Mr. Adams and said sharply, "Karl Adams, I think you are horrid not to let school out. In an hour we won't be able to get home."

Mr. Adams patted Mary on her red hair and said, "Maybe next time, Mary."

Another time in algebra class when Mr. Kirschner gave out the assignment, Betsy blurted out, "Mr. Kirschner, don't you think that assignment is too long, now that spring is here?"

Much to everyone's surprise, he agreed. "All right, Betsy, instead of Exercises 25, 26, and 27, just do 25 and 26." Every one clapped. Betsy was the heroine of the day.

PART

CHAPTER 5

The Depression Hits

*A*fter we graduated from high school, Betsy didn't cross my path for some time. I went to school in Bellingham while Betsy attended the University of Washington. It was then that she dropped the *s* in Betsy and became Betty because she thought it sounded more adult.

Also about that time, Sydney started a tearoom in the University District. Called The Mandarin, it was located in a large colonial building that sat well up off the busy University Avenue. Sydney knew what good cooking was and, although I never ate at The Mandarin, I heard the food was excellent. However, she was no business woman as she had too much heart. Her friends and those of her children would go in to eat, and when they tried to pay the check, Sydney was apt to say, "Oh, Joe, let's make this one on me." She had been the hospitable hostess in her own home too long. She could not make the transition, and the tearoom did not pay.

Some months after The Mandarin closed, on a drive to the Olympic Peninsula, the Bard family was attracted to a picturesque farm. Although Betty's younger brother, Cleve, was only seventeen and had no farming experience, he thought farm life would be wonderful. Practicality was swallowed up in romanticism. They bought the farm. The Bards had many shattering experiences with rural life, but Betty made a joke of them when she told about them later.

Once when Cleve was getting ready to market some tomatoes, he started out with a full truck. A farmer with a load of eggs came barreling out of a side road, and the two trucks collided. Betty said, "It was the finest Spanish omelet ever stirred together in the whole county."

A real tragedy ensued when the government tested the Bards' cows for tuberculosis and shot some twenty-odd in cold blood. Betty did not laugh about this. Later on it was learned there had been a mistake and eventually the government did make some reparations.

One time when Cleve was in Seattle he bumped into an old friend, Bob Heskett, and brought him home to the farm. Both Mary and Betty thought Bob was a beautiful man. He was tall and well-built, with uniform white teeth, dark hair, and blue eyes. In his late twenties, he appeared very smooth indeed to a girl of eighteen. He began to notice Betty rather than Mary, which was most unusual as most of the guys who came to the house were more attracted to Mary. Before the summer was over, the romance had gathered great momentum and Betty confided to me that Bob had finally seduced her in the strawberry patch. We laughed together about that and decided it was a yummy spot in which to be seduced. Bob had already proposed marriage. Soon after, they had a small family wedding with Sylvia Gowen's father, an Episcopal priest, conducting the ceremony. The Gowans were longtime friends of Betty's.

As Betty tells it all so wonderfully in *The Egg and I*, Bob found a chicken ranch for them to buy. When Betty presented me with a copy of the book with a friendly note on the fly leaf, I read it in two sittings. As were thousands of others, I was completely hooked. It was as though I was having a visit with her. She had already told me and groups of friends at parties and showers many of the same stories and it was exciting to see them in print. Recently, however, when I re-read the book for the third time, I was consumed with compassion for her —

having to live with such crude facilities while taking care of two babies and a difficult husband. No wonder Mary had managed to spirit her away when she visited the farm for the last time.

According to Mary, she made a special trip to Chimacum when she knew Bob would not be there. She helped Betty pack her things and those of the girls, Anne and Joan, and they left hurriedly, leaving no word behind. When Betty later contracted tuberculosis, she was thin and worn from that life on the chicken farm, but I never heard her indulge in feeling sorry for herself. Mary brought Betty home to their mother, who was now living in a house on Fifteenth Avenue in Seattle, just south of Sixty-Fifth Northeast and near our old high school.

It was soon thereafter that I met Betty on the Cowan Park streetcar, which ran in front of her mother's home and up to the city reservoir, near where my mother lived. Betty told me then that she was in the throes of a divorce. She told me that Bob had no sense of humor, hung around with crummy friends, and dramatized himself too much. "Furthermore, he wrecked a new car the first day we owned it, and the money for it had come from my grandmother. Since the accident was his fault, we could collect no insurance."

Just before I got off the streetcar she said, "Do you want to hear something funny that Mary said?"

"Of course I do, I've missed hearing all those things," I answered.

Betty quickly began to tell me as it was almost time for her to get off. "A year ago when I was pregnant with Joanie, Mary and I got on the street car. It was very crowded. People were standing and hanging on to the leather straps overhead, swinging and swaying as the car lurched around Lake Union. My stomach was protruding and hitting on the backs of the seats. All at once, without consulting me first, Mary said loudly, 'My

God, isn't there *anyone* going to give a pregnant woman a seat?'"
As Betty prepared to leave the streetcar, she added, "And the
whole streetcar rose in a body to offer me a seat!"

I was teaching school in Auburn, about thirty miles on the
outskirts of Seattle, and every weekend I came home to
Mother's as I didn't know many people in Auburn. During my
surprise meeting with Betty, she had told me Sydney would
love to have me drop by, so I began to stop in to see the Bards
every weekend. I loved the "you-can't-take-it-with-you" atmosphere. Sydney was usually sitting in the corner of the sofa
with a book in one hand, a cigarette in the other, a coffee cup
on the table, and a couple of dogs at her feet. She made me feel
as though she had been sitting there just waiting for me to
come and visit. One of their dogs at the time was Tudor, whom
Betty tells about taking care of in her book, *Onions in the
Stew*. Sometimes Tudor would fight with the other dog, but
Sydney would go right on talking as she quietly shoved the animals out the door.

It was evident that the Bards were feeling the pangs of the
depression. The furniture was getting old and the carpeting a
bit threadbare. There were seven people living there, and only
one of them, Mary, was working. Betty would have to go to
court every now and then to get the support money that Bob
was supposed to be providing.

However, Sydney was still inviting people to stay for dinner even though dinner was only lima beans or rice. She would
season the food well, bring it in on her lovely Wedgewood
marigold platters, and serve it using her ornate serving set. The
atmosphere was that of an elegant dinner party. She never
apologized but carried on in the fashion of the manor-born.

One afternoon when I was there alone with her, a young
man came to the door. Sydney welcomed him in. "Hello, Bill,
come on in and sit down. Just a minute, and I'll get you a cup
of coffee." After she introduced us, she asked if his wife,

Shirley, had had her baby yet, and if he had finished painting the baby's room. Naturally I thought they were old friends. Finally, after he had drunk two cups of coffee, smoked two cigarettes, and warmed his hands at the glowing fire in the fireplace, he cleared his throat. "Well, Syd, I wonder if I could get the $4.00 you owe me for the wood I delivered a couple of weeks ago."

Sydney answered kindly, "I know you need the money, Bill, but I don't have a cent in the house. Mary will be home at four o'clock and she is getting paid today, so if you could drop back this evening I'll have it for you." I didn't dream he was there to collect. After he left, Sydney told me what a sweet young man he was, how fond she was of him, and what good, dry wood he delivered. She concluded, "He doesn't have much of an education, but he is very interesting. He is so different from Leon who was here yesterday and is Mr. Very Dull. Leon, with his Ph.D and all is without a doubt the biggest of bores. He starts to tell you something and he says, 'Yesterday — no, it wasn't yesterday because that is when I went to the dentist — it must have been Tuesday — oh no, that's when I did my laundry.' Finally he gets the time set and he says something like, 'I walked around Green Lake yesterday.' As you know, everyone walks around Green Lake! I'll take a little exaggeration to make a story better than listen to the stark-naked, dull truth."

Weeks later Betty told me that she and Mary had gone to the bank to find out about procuring a mortgage on the house. Betty grinned. "You should have heard what Mary said to this awfully proper banker." Mary was bolder than Betty, as her job selling advertising took her into many inner city offices and board rooms. Of course I wanted to hear.

Betty continued, "We were referred to the vice-president. He was very stiff in his three-piece suit, thick glasses, and highly polished shoes. I was a little overwhelmed when he invited us into his posh office. Heavy green carpets, green leather chairs studded with shiny brass upholstery tacks, and a long mahogany desk across the corner of the room — it was excessive. I think even Mary was a tiny bit uncomfortable in the presence of this financial wizard because she acted quite facetious. When he touched upon the issue of collateral, she interrupted him and said, 'All we have are our two white bodies to offer for that.'

"The banker coughed a dry cough, bit his lower lip, and forced a weak little smile."

Nothing was said about whether or not Betty and Mary got the mortgage. What did that matter when there was a little bit of fun generated? That was the essence of the Bards — they flung convention to the wind and made money seem mundane and secondary to fun in life.

CHAPTER 6

Mary Meets a Body-Thinko

 The Bards had quite an extensive in-family vocabulary, and after being around them for a while, I learned that a *smell-badall* was an obnoxious person of either sex; a *saddo* was a person consumed with self-pity; a *get-in-good-with-the-company* was an apple-polisher; a *body-thinko* talked excessively of his ailments, or was too sexy; a *my-husband-saider* was a woman who quoted her husband constantly and had few ideas of her own; a *pee-pee* talker used barnyard talk and four-letter words; and a *be-happy* was a person not sincerely happy, but one who pretended to be.

Betty had told me early in our friendship that Sydney, and therefore the whole family, had no time for people who told off-color jokes or used vulgar words. They also preferred the scientific names for parts of the body, not the cutesy ones, such as *stomach* rather than *tummy*, *hands* rather than *patties*, and *breasts* rather than *boobs*.

Late one afternoon, Betty and I were sitting in the living room having a cup of tea when Mary came bursting in the front door. "I have just met the most fascinating man. He is a German baron and is in Seattle representing a big diesel firm. He wants to take me dancing Saturday night, and Blanchie, I want you and Betty to get dates and come along with us, as I think Baron von Schlosnagle is a bit of a *body-thinko*. I'll feel safer with him in a group."

Both Betty and I were so flattered that Mary was inviting

*Mary Bard always
had the answers.*

us on a date with her, particularly as she was willing to share a real baron's company with us. I invited Kenn Farnsworth who lived a couple of doors from my mother, whom I had known quite well at one time but hadn't seen much of since I began to teach out of town. I did know, however, that he was a very good dancer. He was reluctant to accept. "The Bards are all screwy," he said. But when I explained that the Baron would be paying for everything, he changed his mind. "Oh hell, why not!"

Betty's date would be Jock Hutchings, an old boyfriend of Mary's who had been dropping by their house of late to visit with Sydney. Mary said she felt sorry for him because his mother was so possessive, and that if it hadn't been for this woman she would still be going with him.

Mary also decided that we should have new dresses. "I have a wonderful contact through the Metzenbaum brothers whose father has a wholesale yardage outlet. They told me anytime I wanted yardage, just let them know." Mary made arrangements to get the material the next morning and we planned to meet in the afternoon to start sewing our dresses. Mary arrived with sparkling eyes, so excited over the wonderful bargain. She unwrapped the package and out came what I thought looked like awning material. She had chosen black-and-white stripes, two inches wide, for herself, yellow-and-white stripes of the same width for Betty — saying it would be perfect with her reddish-brown hair, and blue-and-white stripes for me — "the color of your eyes," said Mary. Her enthusiasm quelled any doubts I might have had that the fabric was inappropriate. The pattern was simple: strapless, with a tight bodice, and long, billowy skirt. Mary said one pattern would fit us all with a few adjustments; "Yours, Blanchie, will have to be quite a bit shorter, of course." As I was well aware that I was not as tall as they, I wondered if two-inch stripes were right for me. But both Betty and I followed right along with anything Mary said. It was her show, after all.

The sewing machine hummed all afternoon and well into the night. I stayed all night and we arose early the next morning to finish the dresses. We tried them on, and since all this sewing had taken place in the living room, occasionally members of the family would walk through. Cleve, Betty's brother, did a double-take. "My God, where is the circus? Sydney, I wouldn't let them out of this house in those tents."

Mary returned, "Well, Cleve, you just don't know what is going on. Stripes are very much the 'in' thing."

And Sydney, the ubiquitous peacemaker, said, "You all look charming and unique. I am quite sure the Baron has never taken out German girls who dressed as strikingly."

When the special evening finally came, Sydney sat in her favorite spot at the end of the sofa, her dogs at her feet. Kenn and Jock were in their dark suits, white shirts, and black bow ties. We girls were grouped together like zebras, waiting for the prey. Suddenly we heard the taxi door slam, and we knew the moment for the pièce de résistance was upon us. Mary answered the knock and said dramatically as she opened the door, "Ah, the Baron!" He looked exactly as we had pictured him: rather portly, with swarthy skin, dark hair, and brown eyes. In his hand he carried a floral box which he presented to Mary as he made a slight bow. The atmosphere was electric as Mary opened the box. "An orchid," she screamed, "and yellow — my favorite! You couldn't have pleased me more." She ran over to Sydney and handed her the corsage pin. "Sydney dear, would you pin it on me? Perhaps right here would be best." She pointed to a spot above her left breast. Against the black-and-white stripes, it gave the effect of an orchid peeking through an iron fence, but Mary's enthusiasm for the occasion overshadowed any incongruity. Such sparkle and verve were a treat for even a baron. Sydney, after pinning the orchid in place, sat silently, smoking her cigarette with a smile on her face. She was highly amused.

The rest of us were standing around like a bunch of stage props. Kenn growled to me under his breath, "I'm just the guy with a big car."

By now, Mary thought it was time to introduce Baron von Schlosnagle. From that moment on throughout the evening, each of us pulled out every German phrase we knew. The men became *Herr* Farnsworth and *Herr* Hutchings. I asked Kenn, who had been to Germany, if we were supposed to use *Herr* with the title of Baron. He didn't answer, but just went on flaunting what little German he had learned while abroad.

We headed for Willard's Roadhouse where the Baron had made reservations. By 1930 most people owned cars and road-houses had begun to spring up all along the main highways. The buildings were attractive by night, but usually a little tacky-looking by day as they were basically night spots. The atmosphere inside Willard's was seductive, with little rose-shaded electric lamps that simulated candlelight on all the tables and windowsills. The orchestra was playing a fox-trot

— "Whispering" — and I felt like dancing immediately. However, we were ushered into our private room and seated at a round table for six. Chicken and steak dinners with French fries and peas were being featured, and although Prohibition was in full swing, there seemed to be plenty of liquor everywhere. Kenn did dance beautifully and soon we were whirling around to the strains of "Sweet Sue, Just You." I was sure of a great evening ahead. But after eating, Kenn began to gripe. "The steak is tough, the music is only second-rate, and I don't believe that guy is a real baron." (Years later Mary told me that without a doubt, the Baron had been a German spy sent to our country to get all the secrets he could before World War II broke out.)

I found it easier to avoid Kenn than listen to his criticisms. About two-thirds into the evening I asked Mary how the Baron was behaving. She answered, "So far he is a perfect gentleman, but his dancing leaves much to be desired."

Betty was enjoying herself because this was her first big night out since she had returned to Seattle from the chicken ranch. She didn't want to cozy up to Jock too much, however, because Mary had warned her about his mother and their too-tidy lifestyle. Besides, Betty was still licking her wounds from her recent broken marriage.

Mary actually was trying to promote a little something between Jock and me and she was not being too subtle about it. She told me how sweet he really was; how he had a good job (in Depression times, that was a real plus); and how he always looked gorgeous in his clothes, and that, as a matter of fact, if I would look in the 1927 *Tyee*, the University of Washington yearbook, I would see a darling picture of him, wearing clothes he had won for being voted "Best Dressed Man on Campus." "Besides, he is a good dancer, having had lessons from the age of ten. He is witty, too, and furthermore," Mary said, "you could handle his mother."

Though Mary did not say it, she inferred that she would like to see the score evened up with Ann Hutchings. Jock was easy to talk with, laughed at my jokes, and asked me to dance two times in a row. Kenn was not enjoying the fun I was having with Jock, and so he set about to drink. When I saw him ask Mary to dance, I was happy because I thought it would make up for the poor dances she had been having with the Baron. While they danced, Jock and I sat at the table and had a good visit. We agreed that the Bard family was quite bohemian, that they were bright, hospitable and always amusing. We both loved Sydney and thought she had done well raising five children single-handedly, and through it all, keeping her serenity and poise.

When Mary and Kenn returned, I eagerly asked, "How did the dance go?" Mary laughed cheerfully. "Blanchie dear, I wanted your presence to protect me from the Baron, and now *your* boyfriend has gotten a little drunk, and he has been trying to do the 'Rape Gavotte' with me." Momentarily, I was nonplused. Most of my contemporaries didn't even know what the word *rape* meant, and in those days if you did, you whispered it behind a raised hand. Mary was open with everything and so uniquely funny I never thought of being shocked — only amused.

When it was time to go home, I suggested that Jock and Betty take Mary and the Baron, and I would drive Kenn's car. He was too drunk to drive; besides, he was furious. He had had a lousy time, and the Baron had not paid his share of the bill. I knew I should be sympathetic since I had promoted his coming, but with the signals of a new romance developing, I found it difficult to empathize. Besides, hadn't Betty and I and our dates been invited to make the evening safe for Mary? And who turned out to be the *body-thinko*? Not Baron von Schlosnagle!

CHAPTER 7

Easter Breakfast

*Q*uite early the next morning after the big evening with Baron von Schlosnagle, Jock phoned and invited me to go with him to visit some friends. He said, "They live on Lake Washington, and you said you like to swim. They have a nice spot and even have a raft with a diving board."

"A raft with a diving board? Oh, I can show you my jackknife dive," I openly bragged. I was anxious to sell my accomplishments.

The host and hostess were Jim and Gerry Hodge, fairly new arrivals to Seattle from Canada, although the Hutchings family had known them for a long time. Their place was small, but looked wonderful on that bright, sunny June day. A soft, green lawn grew down to the sandy beach, and beyond were the sparkling, clear waters of Lake Washington. Mt. Rainier looked down upon all like a fond mother.

Following introductions, Gerry invited us to get into our bathing suits, as she said around noon was the best time of day for swimming. We took her advice and swam awhile and then climbed up on the raft to sun ourselves. We had scarcely stretched out when a man and woman came strolling across the Hodge's front lawn and on down to the water's edge. "Oh, Lord," Jock said, "it's Mother and Dad!" He blushed. His mother cupped her hand beside her mouth and called, "Son, Daddy just drove in from Portland an hour ago, and he has a message for you." Jock excused himself and swam ashore.

Blanche, Dede (Betty's sister), and Betty ready for a swim.

Gerry looked at me. "This doesn't make sense. He lives at home now, since Anne and Ernest moved to Seattle from Spokane. You know Ernest pulled strings and got himself transferred to Seattle so they could be near son Jock. He moved in with them to save money and pay up his bills. My God, they'll see him tonight. I guess I'd better swim in and be friendly." Jim went with her.

I lay there a few minutes wondering if I should go in, too, when Jock called and motioned for me to come. He introduced me to them as a friend of Mary Bard. Anne's eyes fell on my painted toenails and traveled on up to the bottom of my lavender bathing cap. "How do you do, dear? So you are a friend of the Bards? Well, we know Mary." She gave a deprecating little chuckle. "She visited us in our home in Spokane." We chatted for a few minutes until Gerry said, "Let's get back in the water so Jock can hear his message." As we swam back to the raft, Gerry said, "I think she came to check up on you, Blanche."

When I phoned Mary the next day, she blurted immediately, "You have been out with Jock. He phoned me to get your telephone number. Have you met his mother yet?"

When I told her the message story, she answered, "Uh-huh, uh-huh. Typical. See what I mean? But Blanchie, he is a catch and seems ready to settle down. He has a college degree, membership in Zeta Psi fraternity, a job — and don't overlook that darling gray convertible. You know how he can dance! He has taken lessons since the age of ten. Look how handsome he is. You stay in there and pitch. His mother will try to interfere, mark my words."

"Well, Mary, if you think he is such a prize, why aren't you still in there pitching?" I finally asked.

"It's his mother. Let me tell you about my trip to Spokane, followed by the boner I pulled on Easter Sunday last year. Can you meet me at the coffee shop on the 'Ave' at three today?"

"Sure thing," I said, and then remembered my dental appointment. I was really falling for Jock. I hadn't met anyone so far who had such qualifications, and my schoolroom life presented few opportunities to meet any men. Mary was really supportive, so I phoned and cancelled the appointment and hurried down to the University District to our favorite coffee shop.

Soon Mary came whizzing in the door, dressed in a suit and looking businesslike as she had another appointment after ours. She always made an entrance, no matter where she was. Everybody looked up as she strode in, sat beside me, and started to tell her story.

"Jock invited me to spend the weekend with his family in Spokane. We drove up to this lovely, brick house fronted by a perfect lawn; as a matter of fact, it was the most manicured place on the block. As we stepped out of the car, an adorable, perfectly groomed wire-haired terrier named Warbuck bounded out to the car to meet us.

"Inside the house everything was placed on the dotted line — magazines piled on the coffee table according to size, a tidy fire laid in the no-ashes fireplace awaiting the touch of a match, and Oriental rugs placed appropriately. Anne immediately told me that she hired a cleaning woman once a week at which time she went to the beauty shop for a hairdo and a manicure; that she was president of the Weavers' Guild; and that Warbuck had a long and impressive pedigree. Accustomed as I was to our freewheeling lifestyle, I was beginning to feel uncomfortable, wondering if I could possibly measure up to this perfectly run household.

"Anne had a little supper ready for us and as she served the chicken aspic nested in crisp watercress and the German potato salad, she said, 'Son's favorites.' Then she smiled fondly at him as she leaned her head against his.

"I slept in the guest room which was done in pink and white. Dainty, white ruffled curtains dressed up the leaded windows, while a pink bedspread covered the smooth, four-poster mahogany bed. A pretty little Royal Doulton figurine on the dresser picked up the color scheme. Over in a little alcove, a dozen or more pictures of Jock were arranged chronologically from babyhood to a recent pen-and-ink drawing by a well-known Northwest artist. When I went down the next morning to breakfast, Anne announced that we were having Son's favorites again. They were eggs Benedict, ryebread toast with orange marmalade, and, of course, orange juice and coffee.

"Anne told me just before we were to leave for Seattle that they would be coming over at Easter to spend time with Son, and I, in a rush of gratitude, glibly said, 'When you do, Sydney and I would love to have you come for Easter breakfast.'"

Mary drank the last sip of coffee and looked at her watch. "I have just time enough to tell you about the Easter breakfast. Jock is a special agent for an insurance company and travels a great deal. He told me that he would be gone until Easter and would be having a little threesome dinner with his parents on the Saturday before Easter, but they would all see me Easter morning.

"About that time I was becoming well-acquainted with Florence James, wife of Burton James, both of whom were two of the founders of the Seattle Repertory Theatre. Through Florence, I was meeting many of the people involved in the theatre, and several of them started to drop in at our house. Sydney loved having them and always had the ubiquitous cup of coffee ready. She listened to their lively, witty conversation, and was a perfect hostess.

"Well, on the Saturday night before Easter, more than the usual number of new friends dropped by after the performance. Coffee drinking, smoking, and clever chatter were followed by our rolling up the rugs for dancing. Everybody stayed and stayed, and it was well after three a.m. when they left and Sydney, Betty and I dragged ourselves up the stairs to bed.

"It seemed as though I had barely closed my eyes when Betty was shaking my shoulder. 'Mary, wake up, wake up! The Hutchings are down on the front porch, knocking.'

"I told Betty she was having a bad dream, to roll over and go back to sleep. She came back with, 'I am not. Alison just yelled out the window for them to come in, so they must be in the living room by now.'

"All of a sudden, the light began to dawn. I sat upright in bed. 'My God, this is Easter morning. I remember now, I invited them here for breakfast.'

"To which Betty replied, 'Well, you can't serve them coffee. We used it all up last night.'"

Mary continued with her story, laughing and saying, "In retrospect, it is funny, but at the time I felt awful. I threw on the first thing I saw, a filthy sweat shirt and a ragged pair of white dungarees. I went halfway down the stairs leading into the living room, looked over the railing, and there they were, standing by the rolled-up carpet all dressed up in their Easter finery. I had planned to make such a good impression and all was lost.

"Anne was elegant in a navy wool suit, which had been

carefully tailored over her ample bosom. A crisp, white collar peeked discreetly over the neckline. On her large head rested a perky navy straw sailor, trimmed with shiny, plump, dark-red cherries. Ernest, a tad shorter than Anne, was in his navy blue jacket, white trousers, and white suede shoes. He was smiling weakly while nervously twirling his straw hat. Jock stood by looking good enough to eat in a yellow cashmere sweater and gray slacks. He was gazing pathetically up at me. I poured forth my feeble excuse but all I can remember now is that I ended with, 'I'm terribly sorry.'

"Anne said, 'Come on boys, we'll go down to the Meany Hotel and have our Easter breakfast there.' As they strode out the front door without inviting me to go with them, I knew I was washed up in their league. It was almost as though Anne had planned for me to forget, so she could have her boys to herself."

The little episode of the day before made Mary's story all the more convincing. She looked at her watch and said she had to leave that minute or she'd be late to see her client. As I walked out the door with her, I asked, "What makes you have so much confidence in me that you think I can handle that gal?"

"Because you're a teacher and are used to managing difficult cases. She is just like a big spoiled kid, and Blanchie, you've got to get that nice guy out of that trap."

It was as though Mary had failed and now wanted me to try a hand at freeing the victim.

CHAPTER 8

Who Needs Ann Landers?

$\mathcal{A}$fter that Sunday with the Hodges, Jock and I saw each other as much as possible, considering that his job called for much traveling. We dined and danced, shared more swims together, and I met many of his friends. I bought new clothes with abandon, as I was enjoying my attempts to dress up to the Hutchings' standards. Jock liked blue, so I bought blue. My mother had always dressed for occasions, but her theme was "just be sure you are neat, clean, and presentable." Esther, who now had five children, said she was content when the top she was wearing met with the bottom. And my dad, now retired, just didn't want to dress up ever.

When Esther was still living at home and wanted to have friends over for an evening, or if Mother had a P.T.A. committee meeting, they would be sure to tell Dad about it in advance. He knew what they were inferring — that he should put on a tie. But he had rigged up a cozy little retreat by the furnace in the basement. A captain's chair with a faded cretonne pillow, an extension cord with a bright bulb on the end, the morning *Post-Intelligencer,* and his corncob pipe provided a seductive alternative to staying upstairs in a tie with the company. The pipe was a carry-over from when he raised corn on his big farm in southern Indiana, where we were all born.

As far back as I could remember, the only time Dad was completely groomed was on the second Sunday in August, when the whole family went to the Indiana Picnic in Wood-

Jock Hutchings — 1930

lawn Park. Before that Sunday arrived, Mother would check his wardrobe to see if it was intact. When the day came, things started buzzing early in the morning.

To me, the sun shone brighter and the air was sweeter that day, even though the tussle was on to get Dad ready. It was the Indiana Picnic day — a big change in our routine. Mother laid out Dad's clothes, helped him tie his tie, and even checked on the kind of shave he was giving himself. At these times I would tell myself that whoever my husband would be, he was going to like to dress up. And I was sure of Jock's doing just that, for he was well-schooled in all the little social amenities that our family lacked.

Jock not only was turned out properly at all times, he was very attentive as well. This attention was most comforting to me because I had overheard Mother remark to a friend,

"Blanche is a student-type and not really too popular with the opposite sex." I was furious at the time but believed she was right, that I should dedicate my life to teaching school, which she would have loved me to do.

In a few weeks, Jock invited me to go with him and his parents on an insurance excursion to Victoria, British Columbia. The trip on the luxurious *Princess Marguerite* was a treat in itself. Any tour group through Seattle included this trip as part of the package. The pièce de résistance was to have tea at the Empress Hotel, in those days a wonderfully gracious production. The dainty crustless sandwiches, the scalding hot tea poured from highly polished silver teapots, and the stiff linen tablecloths and napkins were "veddy" English and tasteful. (Today you get paper napkins, scores of people waiting in line, and the assembly line ambience of mass production and consumption.)

In the twenties and thirties, professional musicians rendered background music — violin, cello, and piano. At the end of the tea hour the trio played "God Save the King" or "Queen," depending upon whichever was the current ruler. As the first note sounded, the loyal subjects rose to their feet in a body and stood at attention. How the Americans looked forward to joining in this highly British custom!

As we debarked in Victoria, I overheard Ernest say, "Now, Anne dear, let Jock and Blanche do some sightseeing on their own. We can meet them later for tea at the Empress."

When Anne arrived for the tea, Jock leaned over and whispered to me. "Listen to Mother's English accent now when she orders. She becomes more British than Dad was when he married him." (Ernest Hutchings was from Newfoundland.)

On the boat going home, we stood by the railing on the top deck much of the time as the weather was perfect. As we were nearing Seattle, the sun was sinking behind the pale lavender Olympic Mountains, and we watched the lacy foam bounce upwards from the ship's prow as it cut through the blue water.

It was an easy time to feel romantic. Jock took off his Zeta Psi fraternity pin and said, "Hasn't this been a swell day? Look, won't you wear my pin, until I can give you something more permanent — like a diamond?"

"I'd love to," I said spontaneously and gave him a big hug and kiss. I thought, *Gosh, I am going to wear a pin, just like my girlfriends, Marge and Velma.*

When the boat docked in Seattle, all of us were tired. Anne suggested I come home with them so that Son would not have to make the long drive to my house and then go all the way back to theirs. Because of the euphoric state in which I found myself, I would have done anything the Hutchings suggested; soon I would become a member of their family.

Before Anne made me a bed on the sofa in the den, she showed me around their house which had one of Seattle's tremendous views. They had been in this home about three months since their move from Spokane. It was déjà vu for me as Mary had described everything so accurately. After Jock and I did a little proper lovemaking, I nestled into the plump old-rose comforter and drifted off on a pink Cloud Nine. I was supremely happy!

The next day, of course, I dropped in to see Betty and Mary to give them a weekly progress report of my romance. They loved hearing that Ernest had laid down the law to Anne to give Jock and me a little time together. At least he recognized there might be a problem. When I told them about staying all night, Mary pointed out that I was the one who slept on the sofa. Son had not been asked to give up his bed.

"Also," said Mary, "be careful, or she will ask you to stay two or three days. Jock got interested in a gal who taught physical education at Annie Wright's Seminary. She was a very energetic girl with a loud voice. Anne thought the friendship was developing into something more so she invited the girl to spend three days with them. The girl's sergeant's voice and her wish to play tennis most of the day soon made a wreck out of Jock, who was not accustomed to so much exercise and regimentation. He quickly lost interest."

I listened to Mary, but thought, *oh, I can handle that.* Jock invited me to dinner that next Friday, saying it was going to be extra special. He had reserved a table for us in the Georgian Room at the Olympic Hotel. Naturally I was excited and began to live for that evening to come. But later in the afternoon, I had a call from Jock's dad, saying that Jock had to cancel the reservation because he had just driven in from Portland and thought he was coming down with a cold. "Could you come here for dinner instead, if I came over after you?" asked Ernest.

I was disappointed, but what else could I do, the poor guy was sick. Anne had an English dinner — roast beef rare, Yorkshire pudding, Brussels sprouts, and squash. Everything was cooked exactly right and served beautifully by Jock's father. Jock had pulled himself together enough to come to the table and told me that carving a roast properly was part of being an English gentleman, and he was fast learning to do a good job at that. I was impressed over these little extra procedures that the Hutchings deemed important. Many of our family dinners were served on oilcloth at the kitchen table.

Anne apologized for having forgotten the horseradish, and Ernest thought the plates could have been a mite warmer. They expressed the hope that Son felt well enough for a round of bridge after dinner. I spoke up, trying to be funny. "I really don't like bridge, but I do awfully well at Old Maid." There was a stony silence. I realized that if I had said I was going to salute the Hammer and Sickle instead of Old Glory, there would have been less shock. Jock talked me into playing and I began to notice how obvious his efforts were for me to fulfill their expectations.

As the game progressed and I was bravely stating some rules I had learned but was not following, Ernest made a grave error. It was his turn to play and he slapped his card down confidently. There was a short silence, and then Anne yelled, "Daddy, you didn't return my lead, and you have done that two times." Whereupon she swept the cards off the table in one swoop. She was mad! The men knelt to pick up the cards. I was surprised at her anger. My mind flashed back to a time when I was ten years old and had thrown the cards on the floor because my brother was cheating. My mother had said, "Aren't you ashamed to give in to a temper tantrum at your age?"

Anne stalked out of the room, and headed for the stairs. "I'm tired and I am off to bed. Ernest, you had better come too. Give Son and Blanche a little time to visit." In a way, the tantrum was timely for me because I was not enjoying myself, sitting on the edge of my chair, scared I was going to play the wrong card.

Immediately Jock began to talk about the long drive between our houses — thirteen miles to be exact. He had ticked it off on his speedometer. "You know, I've been thinking. June is a long way off, and for us to wait that long to get married sounds terrible. Couldn't we move it up to Christmas? I have a present for you." He reached into his pocket and drew out a purple velvet ring box. "Open it. I hope you like it; it has been in the family, and Mother and Dad gave it to me to give to you."

It was a beautiful diamond in a Tiffany setting. I put my arms around his neck and pulled him down for a kiss, but he turned his cheek and said, "I'm sorry, but I don't want to give you a cold." It was anticlimactic though considerate. I held my left hand out in front of me to admire the ring more fully. Now I was truly engaged.

The next morning Ernest met me as I came into the breakfast room, kissed me and said, "I know you two will be happy." Anne arrived and said she had had a good night and was in a better mood. "Daddy was an old stinker last night the way he didn't return my lead; he knows better than that. Do you like your ring, dear?" Of course I told her it was beautiful and so lovely of them to give it to Jock for me. "Are you happy, dear?" she asked.

I had never been asked that before — everyone had always taken it for granted that I was happy or that if I weren't, it was up to me to do something about it. I didn't want to answer, but if I had to I wanted to say, "No, I am in the dumps!"

When I told Betty about it, she said, "What you should do if she asks you that again is to turn the question on her. Ask her if *she* is happy."

I had suggested to Jock that we just go away some weekend, get married, and then come home and announce it. A lot of stress and work could be avoided that way. I knew my family were not going to throw themselves into a showy wedding, and it meant nothing to me. Jock said, "If we did that it would kill my mother!" Now that I had my diamond and a commitment for marriage at Christmas, I saw that I was going to have to get off Cloud Nine and start wading through some mudpuddles.

I showed my ring to Esther first. She said, "It's beautiful, all right, but I hope you are going to wait for the Depression to lift because no one has any money for clothes, gifts, or anything else."

Dad said, "Whatcha got, Sister? Lordy, how it sparkles. Did Jock give you that?" For a man of few words, he was garrulous. My brother Ralph, nine years my senior, said, "You going to get married? You just quit making mud pies last year and you don't even know where babies come from. Will that ring fit under that catcher's mitt I gave you?"

Brother Carl, thirteen years my senior, had been married for a number of years and was feeling the Depression. He had to get his bit of philosophy into the subject too. "When poverty comes in the door, love flies out the window." He looked at the ring and added, "You say his folks provided the ring. I had to work hard to buy Marge's diamond."

I could have predicted my mother's reaction. Ever since I was in high school and proved to be a good student, she held up her favorite teachers as models for me. She referred to them as "maiden ladies." Miss Anna Meyers and Miss Ida Greathouse were their names, which she never shortened when she spoke of them. Her photograph album bulged with their pictures.

In one photograph, Miss Anna Meyers was dressed in a white embroidered dress with a high neck, long, full skirt, tight sleeves, and a rose tucked into the belt that circled her wasp waist. Her long hair puffed out, framing a sweet face with dainty features. She held a rolled-up diploma tied with a ribbon in her right hand while her left hand was placed on the back of a Duncan-Phyfe chair.

My mother had several pictures of Miss Ida Greathouse. In one photo taken in her classroom, Miss Ida Greathouse wore a white blouse with ruching at the neck and three-quarter-length puffed sleeves tucked into a long, full, navy serge skirt. "Beautiful material and perfectly fitted," my mother said. "Of course, she wore it all year."

"I feel sorry for her having to step into that same outfit every morning. Didn't it get dirty?" I asked.

"She thought of that — she had another one made just like it."

"Then I feel sorry for the kids having to look at that same outfit day after day all year," I answered.

"Oh," said Mother loftily, "these women were intelligent and dedicated to their craft. Their clothes were merely a tasteful covering, while they radiated their beautiful characters and shared their vast knowledge with their students."

I had heard of mothers who were anxious to marry off their daughters — but not mine. She wanted me to be committed to my profession. "It is a very pretty ring though, dear," she said, as she descended from her ivory tower. "However, you haven't known Jock Hutchings very long — don't you think you are rushing things?"

To entertain for a minute the thought that my family would dive enthusiastically into a fancy wedding would be pure fantasy. "You would be better off to take the money you would spend for the wedding and use it as a down payment on a house," they said.

I was facing a dilemma. It was time for me to meet with Betty and Mary. When I told them what was going on, Mary said, "I love the way your family refuses to be impressed by the Hutchings' scheme of things."

"At this point, I wish they were somewhat impressed and willing to meet with some of their terms, at least halfway," I answered.

"Mary and I will help get you through all this stuff that some people think is necessary in order to be really married," Betty said. "We know how to make wonderful open-faced sandwiches. We made some for Mrs. Levenslater's fiftieth wedding anniversary."

"And we'll help you plan a big announcement party that will sweep Anne Hutchings off her feet," Mary added.

"Oh, that is so heartening, because even though my mother is awfully well-read, social events have never interested her. I've been raised on the quotes she knows from Dickens, Bobby Burns, and Shakespeare, such as 'Barkis is willin,' 'Et tu Brute,' and 'Oh wad some power the giftie gie us to see oursels as other see us!'"

I felt apologetic at the moment for Mother's lack of social know-how and went on. "And she is not afraid of anything — even picks up spiders in her bare hands, calls them 'Little Arachnes' and puts them on the back porch. But you mention a party for her to give, and she panics."

Mary said, "One of the guys at the Repertory Theatre told me his father just got in a whole carload of party dresses, and that I can take you and Betty down to pick out something pretty and wholesale. We'll get new dresses and show Anne Hutchings she is not the only one who has clothes! Cheer up, Blanchie."

I climbed back up on Cloud Nine and went home.

CHAPTER 9

Betty Tells Chicken Ranch Stories

*S*ince I was the last offspring to leave the Hamilton nest, Mother had a few hurdles to overcome. As Ralph was often prone to say to me, "With you, Mom is like an old hen with one chicken!" Mother and I were close, as I had fulfilled most of her dreams — until now. She talked little about the coming marriage. However, when I told her that Betty and Mary were going to take over, more or less, by making the sandwiches and arranging for new dresses, she relaxed and began to ask a few questions about the plans we had made.

Marie Sandall offered their new home for the announcement party. The Sandalls were neighbors and old friends. Her father, a builder, had moved the Victorian house in which he and Mrs. Sandall had raised eleven children to a side street, leaving prime view property on which to build the new house. The site overlooked not only the city reservoir and its park, but the University District and Mt. Rainier in all its glory. Marie said, "We have waited for over twenty years for this new home and now we would like to show if off. Furthermore, if you'll provide the chicken, I'll make a chicken salad."

Mother liked these arrangements because she had been raising White Leghorn hens and she could easily contribute the chicken. Betty gave me a list of things to buy for the refreshments. She and Mary turned the white sandwich bread, green peppers, asparagus spears, shrimp, cucumbers, and stuffed olives into beautiful works of art. Mother watched them closely as they worked in her kitchen. "They are performing miracles with that food," she marveled. She herself was a meat-potato-pie cook, always attempting not only to please Dad but to fill him up. The eye appeal of food had never occurred to her. She was a little distressed over the way the girls were wasting crusts, but she surreptitiously brushed them into a paper sack to be made into bread pudding later that day.

A week before the party, Mary took Betty and me to the wholesale house to pick out our dresses. She chose soft green, Betty, yellow, and I, blue, of course. The dresses were made of filmy chiffon with scoop necks, big three-quarter sleeves, and flowing long skirts with attached slips underneath. Their styles varied but all three were extremely feminine. I think the dresses made us so very confident that we floated in and out among the guests feeling like the most important people in Seattle. Betty was laid back as she quietly sized up people and situations that we later hashed over and enjoyed again. Mary, with her usual flare for life, made funny remarks and gave the occasion a dimension it needed.

Anne had suggested that a beautiful way to announce the engagement would be to give each person a rosebud with our names entwined in hearts tucked into the petals, but even as I was telling this to Betty, she rummaged through her sewing basket and picked up a colorful little horn — the kind blown at New Years' parties. When she blew on it, there was a toot and then out furled twelve inches of double tissue paper about an inch wide with yellow feathers on the end. "Let me try it," I said. I blew the horn and and discovered that as long as I held my breath it stayed extended.

Betty said spontaneously, "Look, you could have 'Jock and Blanche' printed on that rolled-up paper and give one to everyone as a favor. When they blow, they will see your names."

"Wonderful — it will add a little pizzazz to the party."

We found two dozen at the trick store down on First Avenue.

Almost all the guests at the party were very much surprised at the announcement, as the courtship had been of whirlwind proportions.

Velma and Marge came to me and said, "This isn't fair, we've been going with our men for over a year and neither of them will think of marriage until the Depression is over." Their men were the practical kind — my Jock was romantic!

Mary and Anne behaved like old buddies. Mary sat at Anne's knee with her filmy green skirt spread around her like a lily pad. Anne gazed down at her, apparently entranced with what Mary was saying.

Betty looked at me and said, "Mary's over there out-dramatizing Anne."

I answered, "Mary is doing so well, why would she ever think I could do any better than that with Anne?"

Betty, always the discerning one, said, "The reason they are getting on so well is that Mary no longer poses a threat."

When I went to the Bard's the next day to give the girls perfume as a gesture of gratitude for all they had done, Sydney said, "I want to give you something. I know how you always admired my Wedgewood platters, and times being what they are, I can't afford to buy a present." She reached down to the floor near the dining table, picked up a platter, and went to the sink to run hot water over it. "I hope you don't mind the dog's having used it; he just finished the left-over meatloaf."

Since I had always loved the way Sydney treated her dogs like humans, this was a perfect way to be presented with a wedding gift from her. When I told Betty that this reminded me of one of Mother's famous stories, she said, "Your mother always has a story for everything. C'mon, let's hear it!"

"The lord and master of the manor said to his humble servant, as he placed a dish of food in front of him, 'Knave, is this dish clean?' The servant answered, 'Yes, me lord, as clean as Three Waters can make it.' Later in the day, the master heard the servant call his dog. 'Come here, Three Waters, and clean the master's plate.'"

Sydney's gift was exactly the right thing. The platter always has had an important spot on the walls of the various dining rooms in the many places we have lived.

In due course, after our engagement party came the showers. At one of them the hostess had planned some games. For the first game she gave each guest a sheet of paper with a list of words connected with a marriage. The letters were scrambled out of place. Betty was the first to turn in a completed list of correct words, and won the prize.

As she accepted it, she said, "This is quite different from the last party I went to up on the ranch. One of Bob's undesirable friends invited us and I said I wouldn't go. Bob knew how I felt about those people and yet he insisted that I go with him. His method of getting me to consent was to pour a cup of kerosene on the back porch and then hold a lighted match about ten inches above it. 'You'll go, or I'll drop this match,' he said. Knowing Bob, I thought I had better say I would. I went with him and had a terrible time." Betty laughed as she told us about this experience, and in no way sounded the martyr.

This story led to others, and we heard about the bats that flew in through the bedroom windows; the outhouse at night; ice in the henhouse; and her neighbors whom she actually enjoyed because they were so different.

Soon after our marriage, Mary found her doctor to marry, and as she tells it in *The Doctor Wears Three Faces,* she was the one who went in pursuit. Before long there were showers for Mary, who said, "My hostesses didn't plan games; they counted on Betty to entertain us with her stories of life on the ranch."

When the time came for Betty to write her best seller, *The Egg and I,* her material was all stored, ready to crack the eggshell and burst into life.

CHAPTER 10

Who Won Round One?

*J*ock loved hearing the way the announcement party had gone, especially the fact that Mary and Anne had hit it off so well. He liked the hilarity of all the blowing horns celebrating our engagement. But he became quiet after laughing over the party and soon said, "How about moving up the date to Thanksgiving? Christmas will never come."

My answer was a repetition of what I had said before. "Jock, I keep saying I am anxious to get ceremonies all behind us, and my family is in no mood for a fancy wedding. I have no money saved to pay for it, my dad is retired, and he and Mother live frugally on his income. Carl is out of a job, Esther's husband is supporting five kids with no job, and Ralph (a professional ball player at the time) doesn't even want me to get married because he won't have anyone to practice pitching to anymore. Couldn't we just go to Bremerton or somewhere else out of this county, come home, and quietly announce that we are married?"

"It would kill my mother! Right now she is asking me where we shall be getting married and where the reception will be and all."

"Okay, then you come up with a plan and I'll see how it goes with my family."

September came, school was starting, and I had to get my apartment prepared for my residency during the school week. The apartment was at Redondo Beach, near Tacoma, a beautiful part of Puget Sound, and had three rooms: a kitchen, bedroom and huge living room with a fireplace. Until January, I would take a swim after school and then come in and dress in front of a roaring fire. I liked the lifestyle and my rent was only ten dollars a month, including wood for the fire.

Jock was on a three-week business trip which gave me ample time to start the school year. However, he phoned a few days before I expected him home and said he would be out for dinner. I was surprised and delighted. Just before he arrived, I found myself breathless and excited. His mother had asked me several times if I really loved her son and I resented it, but it did make me examine myself for any "in-love" symptoms. I felt I had some, but said to myself, I'm not going to run and tell Anne. I remembered what Betty had said. "You don't have to answer that question; that is between you and Jock."

I built a big fire in the fireplace, put up a card table, and set it with some bright-colored pottery which I had been collecting, thinking of my intended life of domesticity. My centerpiece was one candle encircled with russet button chrysanthemums. I had never done much cooking, as becoming a housewife had not been a goal until recently. I put on a fluffy little organdy apron and tried an easy recipe for baked pork chops. Scalloped potatoes and peas rounded out the menu.

Before we sat down to eat, I inveigled Jock into having a quick swim with me, and when I finally served the food, he was radiant over our little tête-a-tête. After dinner, we indulged in a little lovemaking but it was all very proper as Jock said he wanted to keep the intimacies of lovemaking for our marriage. I knew Mother would approve of this gentlemanly approach. He did say, "Let's move our marriage up to November 11 — Armistice Day — as it will be a three-day weekend. I want you to know that I've explained to Mother and Dad about there being a Depression and how it wouldn't be fair to involve people in an expensive ceremony and reception. I told them that we

both like the St. Mark's Chapel on Broadway. We can skip send-
ing formal invitations, and afterwards can send out engraved
announcements. Anyone who likes may come to the chapel."
It sounded reasonable to me, but I did ask, "Are you sure your
parents are satisfied with these arrangements?"

He answered, "Well, more or less."

The week before the wedding, we had to go to Port
Orchard in Kitsap County to get our license because if we got
it in King County, it would be listed in the newspapers and I
would lose my teaching job — no married teachers were
allowed in those days. I wanted to finish out the year.

Esther reluctantly agreed to be my matron of honor, but
Ernest was most pleased that Jock had asked him to be his best
man. Esther said she was flattered that I wanted her but she
was worried over what to wear. She had no money for a new
dress. Carl consented to give me away when Dad refused to
participate — he had already done his dressing-up for 1932
when we went to the Indiana Picnic.

As it was to be an informal, fall evening wedding, I did not
plan to wear a traditional white wedding dress. I went to I.
Magnin's so that whatever I chose would be quality. I bought
the most expensive dress I had ever owned — it cost sixty-five
dollars. In those days you paid a nickel for an ice cream cone
and the butcher gave you a wiener when you bought thirty-five
cents' worth of round steak. The saleslady understood the
atmosphere we were trying to create and recommended the
heavy-textured brown silk crepe dress trimmed in eggshell satin.
She suggested brown suede high heel pumps trimmed in a
modest iridescent leather to match. I felt comfortable with the
ensemble, and Mother approved because it was something that
could be worn for many occasions in the future.

Greta, my hairdresser, an old friend from grammar school
days, had been bleaching my hair and giving me other beauty
hints for about a year. We carefully referred to the bleach as a

"rinse" as the former word had a risqué connotation. My principal at school had noticed my hair was lighter, but since he liked it, said he would defend me to any parents who might mention it. I said, "Tell them it is caused by salt water and sun!" He was happy with that explanation. Greta wanted to do something a little extra for me now that I was getting married, so at her suggestion, I let her dye my eyelashes. She said that with blond hair, black eyelashes would be smashing. However, when Esther saw my dyed eyelashes, she said, "My Lord, now what have you done to yourself? The bleached hair was extreme enough, but now you are a real hussy!"

"Jock likes it," I said.

"Well, ever since you came to my garden party with your toenails painted bright red and pink sandals on your feet, I am prepared for anything."

The truth was, my painted toenails had livened up a pretty dull party. Esther's bantam chickens had the run of the yard, and every time I sat still, the bantam chicks pecked at my toenails, thinking they were kernels of bright Indian corn. It set most of the prim little ladies to laughing.

We still hadn't worked out what Esther would wear. As I look back on it, I realize I should have bought her a dress. After all, I had a job. But I was in a very self-centered stage of my life. At the last minute, Inez, one of the very few of Esther's close friends who had a job, offered to loan her a rich, dark green silk dress which went well with my brown one. When Esther tried the dress on, Inez said, "It suits you much better than it does me — I'll just give it to you as a wedding present for Blanche."

Things began to move along quite well, or at least I thought they were, considering that the two families were at opposite ends of the spectrum in terms of what they thought a wedding should be. Ceremonies had always struck my funny bone, and when I was a Camp Fire girl at candlelighting ceremonies, I giggled all the way through each performance. Now to be the center of the biggest ceremony of my life was a sacrifice, but one I was willing to make in order to land this adorable guy.

But there was rough water ahead. I was not too surprised when, a week before the wedding, Jock phoned and asked if I could come by their house as his mother was upset. He refused to talk much over the phone but pleaded with me to come. Since it was Friday and I would be driving into town from the beach anyhow, I swung around to Alki, parked my pretty little Ford roadster in front of their stately brick house on Admiral Way, and approached the front door. Ernest greeted me with a kiss, saying, "Dear, we are a little upset here. Mother is upstairs in bed and Son is down in the garage. Both are extremely frustrated. Maybe you had better go downstairs first."

Jock was pacing up and down in the garage in tears. I stood in the doorway and watched. "What on earth is the trouble?"

"Mother doesn't like our wedding plans after all," he said. "She feels she is not included in anything, and she doesn't know what is going on. Would you please go and talk to her?"

"But you told me she was satisfied with everything," I said.

"I thought she was, but she got to mulling it over and started to feel sorry for herself — you know, the time is getting closer and I think things suddenly closed in on her. I hate my mother! She ruins more things I try to do," Jock said plaintively.

I felt very sorry for him, but the last thing I wanted to do was to go up and beard the lioness in her den. How ironic that one family did not want to be included, considered it a chore, while the other family felt left out.

"Well, all right, I'll do it for you." I slowly walked up the basement stairs to the entrance hall. I looked at the stairs that led up to Anne. I looked out the front door at my little Ford roadster with the top down — one of my dreams come true. It was only four months old. I could save myself plenty of grief if I ran out the front door, jumped into my car, and drove away.

Then I thought of Miss Ida Greathouse and her schoolroom uniforms — is that what I wanted for myself? Next I remembered what Mary had predicted. "As the wedding date draws nearer, the jaws of the steel trap will grow tighter, but you stick with it," she had said. "Don't let her beat you out of her Jock. It will be one of the kindest things you have ever done."

I plodded up the stairs which were heavily carpeted with a thick, luxurious Oriental runner. I stood at the open door of Anne's room. She was wearing a white satin bed jacket, and looked like a small mountain sitting there in bed. The usually perfectly coifed hair was disheveled, she wore no make-up, her eyes were swollen, and tears stained her cheeks. I made myself step into that room, and tried my best to sound compassionate. "Anne, are you all right?"

She wiped her eyes with a man's white handkerchief and sobbed inconsolably. "No, I certainly am not. I don't know what is going on and I am being kept completely in the dark about the wedding."

"It was my understanding that Jock had made the plans with Ernest's and your approval. But this is what we are hoping to do. Since my family is feeling the Depression and many of our friends are too, we are not indulging in the usual frills of a fancy wedding."

When I finished, she sounded like a child who had been denied a ride on the merry-go-round, and asked for a bag of popcorn instead. "Couldn't Daddy and I have a little party here after the ceremony?"

"The announcement party was to take the place of that, and anyhow, Jock says it is not proper for the groom's family to give a party," I answered.

"Oh, he says that, does he? Well, I happen to know it has been done. When Ernest and I were married in Chicago, my brother Phil provided a coach and four to take us to the church and fetch us to his home afterwards for a beautiful reception."

What I felt like saying was, "To hell with the coach and four — it's all my brother can do to get a decent pair of shoes to walk me down the aisle." Instead, after a hard swallow, I said, "Wasn't that a wonderful brother! I don't have that kind."

At this point, again I heard Mary whispering in my ear, "You can handle Anne — you can handle Jock's mother." I needed that message.

Finally I laid my cards on the table. "Anne, I wanted to elope and cause no one trouble, but Jock said no, he couldn't do that to his mother. I view what we are doing as a compromise. If you want to have a party later, I see no reason why you shouldn't."

"Did Son really say he couldn't do that to his mother?" Anne asked, with a tiny bit of cheer in her voice. She had found a straw to grasp. Then she cast her eyes to the ceiling and said woefully, "At least he has considered me!" She seemed to be consoled now that she was aware that she had been thought of by her only child whom a younger woman was usurping from her.

I was relieved that part of the battle was over. "I'm going to find Jock and tell him you are feeling better." I fled from the room with visions of escaping in a coach and four. Soon Anne slipped on her robe and Jock left his garage sanctuary and we all gathered in the living room — one happy family.

CHAPTER 11

Married or Not

*E*arly the next morning Jock phoned. "Are you still willing to marry me on November 11?"

"Yes, by all means, yes! Now more than ever I am determined that we should continue on as planned." I had thought a lot about the episode of the evening before and my dander was up. This time, I didn't even check with Betty or Mary about how to proceed. I had picked up the gauntlet myself and needed no more prodding from anyone. I was now dedicated to wresting this nice fellow from the clutches of his possessive mother.

Jock continued, "I have a form here from St. Mark's that we have to fill out, but you hurried away before I had a chance to tell you about it. Mother is feeling pacified today and will phone you later."

I didn't know whether I was ready to talk to her or not, but I knew we should keep the lines of communications open. I didn't tell my mother what had happened as she would have been intolerant of such goings-on, and more than that, she would have been offended that anyone should hesitate for a moment to want her son to marry my mother's last little chick.

Soon the phone rang. It was Anne. I told myself to act as though nothing had happened, to be pleasant, even charming.

"Blanche, dear," she started out, "I am feeling much better today, and Daddy and I would like to have you and Son join us for dinner at the Athletic Club tonight." She had assumed a melodic tone of voice filled with pumped-up cheer. You would never guess this to be the same distraught woman of yesterday, sobbing into the man's handkerchief.

"I'd love to go. I love eating at the Athletic Club, and I hear the new chef is excellent." I tried to measure charm for charm, using the same kind of voice Anne had used.

We all met at six-thirty, dressed in our best clothes, of course, and determined to be jolly, witty, and loving. After dinner, Jock pulled out the blank official form from St. Mark's. One of the questions asked if we had been baptized. Of course Jock had been, and in the Episcopal church, but I had not. When I was born, we lived in a little town in Indiana where the people were mostly Methodists or Catholics. Mother had often told me that she and her mother and father had all joined the Universalist Church when they were living in Pasadena; she loved the church because they believed in universal salvation. Much to her disappointment, when they returned to Rockport, Indiana, there was no Universalist church. Dad was a Methodist, so they were married by a Methodist minister, but Mother could not accept the Methodists' belief in hell fire and damnation. Therefore, she attended no church, and when it came to having babies baptized, she chose not to.

When I spoke up and admitted that I had never been baptized, the conversation stopped for a moment. Then Anne drew herself up to her maximum height, put her hand on her hip and said authoritatively, "Just leave it blank — it is none of their business anyhow." All at once Anne was on my side, helping to get the wheels of marriage turning. I did as I was bade, but I always wondered if maybe a *yes* had been filled in later, before the document was returned to the church.

Than another obstacle arose. Jock had been married for about six months to a gorgeous campus beauty, some few years back. Mary had told me about it. "Each one of them thought the other had money with which they could finish college. However, both sets of parents refused to support them, so

Blanche's betrothal announcement. (Courtesy of the Seattle Times.)

they quickly severed the marriage."

When the question on marriage was read, it was my turn to score. I could truthfully say no, I had never been married. Poor Jock was stymied — but only for a moment. Anne cleared her throat and said firmly, "Never mind answering that question. What they don't know won't hurt them." She laid her eyes on me and I felt certain they were saying, *that goes for you, too.*

Both Anne and Jock were set on our marriage taking place in the chapel at St. Mark's. There was something socially correct about being married in this Episcopal chapel, and it was about the only part of our plans of which Anne totally approved. She was not about to let a few church rules stand in the way. Years later, when I thought of our vows being taken under false pretenses, I wondered if we were truly married, and if our kids were really legitimate.

The rest of the evening was play-acting; everyone laughed heartily over what the other one said. Perhaps the disturbance of the previous day had cleared the atmosphere, but if Betty could have listened in on us, I am sure she would have said, "What a bunch of old *be-happys!*"

On Friday evening, November 11, at St. Mark's Chapel,

Married or Not

Katherine Blanche Hamilton and George Keith Hutchings were joined in holy matrimony by Dean John McLauchlan. The chapel, beautiful in its own right, was made even more so by a large, handsome brass container on the altar. It was filled with autumn leaves, brown with splashes of orange, green, and yellow. Later I learned that it had been put there that afternoon by Mary and Betty.

Jock, his dad, and my brother, Carl, wore their dark suits. Carl complained all the way to the church about the cheap shoes he had bought; they were stiff and pinched every one of his toes. He threatened to walk down the aisle stocking-footed, if the pain didn't ease. Esther and I were in our green and brown silk dresses. I hadn't seen Esther in anything but housedresses for so long and thought she looked wonderful.

Esther had said it would be a poor excuse of a wedding with no music, so at the last minute I asked my friend, Audrey Tuthill, who had a beautiful contralto voice, to sing Grieg's "I Love Thee" and "I Love you Truly" by MacDowell.

As I walked down the aisle on Carl's arm, I surreptitiously glanced down and saw he had on his shoes and wasn't even limping. Obviously, he had been teasing. I spotted Mary and Betty sitting in a pew toward the back. Mary had a smug look and Betty was smiling broadly. As Dean McLauchlan performed the service, I gazed steadily into his sparkly eyes. I was sure he was clairvoyant and could see me as an unbaptized woman and Jock as a divorced man, but was good sport enough to go along with our game.

After the final pronouncement that we were man and wife, we hurried down the aisle out to the waiting cab. Mary made a little circle with her thumb and forefinger — I knew she meant "victory at last!"

It had not been easy.

CHAPTER 12

Hairpins and Purple Lupine

*J*ock and I agreed that we should live on the salt water, and since my little place at Redondo was too far for him to drive, we compromised and moved to Three Tree Point. Each of us would have to drive twelve miles to work; he, to the Exchange Building in the heart of Seattle and I, to Federal Way. We loved the place that we had found together. The front deck acted as a seawall, and at high tide the water rose about halfway up. French doors led from the living room to the deck, along which was a glassed-in sleeping porch where we were either lulled to sleep in mild weather by the slap, slap, slap of rhythmic waves, or kept awake in stormy weather by the crash-bang of big breakers.

The living room was square with a rustic stone fireplace on one side. In front of it, double springs and a mattress rested on short legs. Over this we threw a huge India-print spread and on top of that we heaped piles of pillows. It was an inviting spot on which to stretch out and relax in front of a crackling fire. At the other side of the room was our dining area and as we sat at the table, we watched an intermittent parade of boats of every size and type. There was also a small bedroom. The kitchen was the least appealing room, but a kitchen held no priority for me at that stage. The house was a newlywed's dream.

The Tuesday following our wedding, I returned to my first- grade classroom and had the usual strenuous day with my little kids. As I drove home I pictured the first-class homemaker I planned to be once I stepped into the house. What a dreamer I was! Jock had asked for a meat pie to be made out of the leftover pot roast. I felt smug that I knew how to make one, although I had never really done it before. Once that was in the oven, I would sprinkle Jock's shirts and try my hand at ironing. Anne had proudly told me that she, herself, ironed both of her boys' shirts.

First I slipped out of my school clothes into a pair of pale blue silk lounging pajamas Mother had made me as part of my scanty trousseau. I thought them most appropriate for this seaside setting as they had a sailor collar. I sprinkled the shirts, rolled them up in a bath towel, and proceeded with the pie. After reading the directions on the Bisquick box for making crust, I realized I had no rolling pin. I snatched a can of corn off the shelf, its only qualification for a rolling pin its roundness. Quickly I wiped it off and rolled out the crust. It worked, but left an ugly imprint on the dough as I had failed to remove the label. All this time I was trying to make the fire go in the wood stove, but it was spitting at me stubbornly, complaining about the wood which was not only green, but wet.

When at last I got the meat pie in the oven I set up the ironing board and started on the shirt collar, as Anne had said to do. Something went wrong; the iron stuck to the starch on the collar. My eyes were getting red from the smoky stove, tears were rolling down my face, and my nose was starting to run when Jock popped in the door.

"Surprise!" he called. "I came home early. This is our first real day of being married and I could hardly wait to get here." Instead of his lovely blond bride with black eyelashes greeting him with a big kiss while a meat pie quietly baked in a hot oven and the smell of freshly ironed shirts filled the air, he stepped into a room filled with blue smoke, an unbaked pie in a cold oven, and a shirt wrinkled and scorched, still on the ironing board.

We went to a little hamburger stand for dinner. Both of us were getting our first taste of marriage disillusion.

We quickly learned that we needed some help. It never occurred to either of us that with both of us working, we might share the household duties. If a woman chose to work in 1932, fine, but that didn't mean the household was not her entire responsibility as well. Our landlady found us a strong woman who would clean the house, do the washing and ironing, and put a meal in the oven to be ready when we got home. She charged fifty cents an hour. Along with this marvel, we bought an electric plate. Now I could come home, put on my seductive pretties, and sprawl on our studio couch in front of the fire. We also got some dry wood. I was learning so much all at once. Foremost, I learned that marriage had more to it than an exciting companion with whom you did nothing but dance, swim, and have fun.

Anne had resigned herself to the fact that we were married, and we usually ate dinner with her and Ernest once a week. As to Betty and Mary, we weren't seeing much of them now, as Three Tree Point was a long way from the University District. Mary was dating her doctor, Clyde Jensen, and learning that when one tried to make social plans including a doctor, flexibility was a must.

One late Sunday afternoon, however, Mary dropped by to see us. She was aglow. Her eyes were shiny and her curly auburn hair bounced on the shoulders of her tweed coat. Her arms were filled with long spears of purple lupine. "Jens and I have had a wonderful day. We picnicked first, and then walked to this gorgeous hillside covered with lupine."

She interrupted herself to ask for the pretty green vase we had received as a wedding present. While Jock went to fetch it, she said to me as an aside, "When I found a particularly pretty little spot, I sat down and all the hairpins just happened to slip out of my hair. The color of my hair had to look elegant with the purple lupine all around. I was trying to look irresistible. That was my goal."

One of the fascinating things about both Mary and Betty was that they exposed their idiosyncrasies and laughed over them.

Mary arranged the flowers, placed them in front of a mirror, and waved good-bye as she sped off to Jens who waited in the car, as he was on his way to an appointment. Whether it was the flowing copper hair in the purple lupine or Mary's other intriguing ways, she and Dr. Clyde Jensen were married shortly after that.

Betty had taken a job with the National Recovery Administration. It was in the Exchange Building, the same place where Jock's offices were located. Whenever I went to his office, Betty and I would have coffee together. Usually I would be there to help Jock get out some important mail. Betty would drop by and say, "How about it, Simon Legree, could you spare the 'little woman' for a few minutes to have coffee with me?"

Her approach always worked because Jock was amused by the way she had him tagged as a slave driver. He went along with his part and reluctantly said I could go. Over coffee, Betty would tell me all about the characters with whom she worked and I would try to match her tales with stories of my cronies.

Betty was dating these days and Sydney was always there to take care of Anne and Joan, Betty's daughters. Mary confided to me, however, that Betty would have a hard time finding a man as smart as she. "Right now she is going out with one of Seattle's most brilliant electrical engineers, and I worry that soon she will have him thinking he can't put two wires together. She is so above the little feminine foibles that men adore in a woman."

I loved the way Mary always had the answers, and expressed them so colorfully.

CHAPTER 13

Sydney–A Real Friend

$\mathcal{A}$lmost three years after our marriage, I became pregnant with our first child. We now lived in the Green Lake district. We wanted the right environment for our baby, and the area around Green Lake had good places to walk and a big wading pool surrounded by expansive lawns and trees. Several of my old friends were living there, now starting their own families as well. And of course my mother, who had said she would be happy to baby-sit anytime, was nearby. Likewise we were not far from the Bards once again. Walking was recommended then, as now, for pregnant women, and one of my favorite walks was to the Bards' so I could visit with Sydney. The round trip was about three miles. I walked during the day while Betty was at work and her children were in school, and it was during that period I really got to know Sydney. Her contentment with her life was a good influence on me at the time.

Sometimes I found her digging in her garden or baking a cake in the big kitchen oven. Most of the time, especially in bad weather, she would be snuggled in her spot on the sofa, book in hand. She was fond of Galsworthy's writings and told me she had re-read his *Forsyte Saga* many times.

Often I had cooking questions to ask her. Not only was she a super cook, she could turn out a tasty full meal while visiting with me, a feat I have never been able to master. Recently, I had more proof of this. I bragged to a house guest about my wonderful carrot cake recipe. "I'll make one for the picnic at

Jill's (my now-adult daughter) tomorrow." As we visited, I grated the carrots, my least favorite part of making this cake, and stashed them away in the refrigerator. Then I put the rest of the ingredients together, all the while chatting with my guest about old times in Green Lake.

I was relieved when I placed the cake in the oven, set the timer, and sat down for a cup of tea and uninterrupted visiting. The cake looked great when I took it out of the oven. When I turned it onto the cooling rack I noticed there wasn't a crumb left inside the pan. Jill was delighted when I arrived with this special treat. Later, however, when she took the first bite, she said, "Mother, this cake is not up to your usual standard."

"It's got to be," I answered in defense, "I followed the directions precisely." But when I tasted it, I knew Jill was right. My house guest was noncommittal, and the cake was not popular. The next afternoon when my friend reached into the refrigerator for a cold drink, she brought out a four-cup pitcher filled with grated carrots. "What are you saving these for?"

Obviously, I cannot visit and bake at the same time. But the recipe is good, although I guarantee you will not like the cake unless you remember the grated carrots!

Blanche Caffiere's Carrot Cake

Blend: 2 c. sugar & 1 ⅓ c. salad oil
Add: 4 eggs, beaten
Sift: 2 c. flour, 2 tsp. baking soda, ½ tsp. cinnamon, 2 tsp. baking powder, & pinch of salt
Add: 4 c. grated carrots & ¾ c. chopped walnuts to wet ingredients
Blend: all ingredients well
Bake: in a well-greased, floured Bundt pan @ 350° for 50—60 min.

Frosting

Blend: 8 oz. cream cheese & ½ lb. butter, softened
Add: 1 lb. powdered sugar
Flavor: with 1 T. grated orange peel & 2 T. orange juice
Blend: all together until very smooth

Sydney once said to me, "Ask me anything you want about cooking, gardening, or books, but never ask me about house-cleaning. My mother was an immaculate housekeeper to the point that it was a fetish with her. I vowed I would never make it my priority." That helped account for the free and welcome atmosphere always present at the Bards'.

Once I told Sydney how much I liked her name, that it had a classical ring, and she surprised me by saying that she had been Elsie Sanderson up until her marriage to Darsie. Neither one of them liked the name *Elsie,* and therefore mulled over a name-change. Elsie's father and grandfather had been called Sydney, a name she and Darsie both liked. Henceforth she would be Sydney.

"How did you ever happen to meet Darsie?" I asked spontaneously. Whenever Sydney referred to her late husband, I always sensed what great love and admiration she had for him. She was an Eastern girl from a proper, sedate family, while Darsie was a true Westerner from Oregon.

Sydney seemed pleased to tell their story. "Darsie had come East to attend Harvard and study geology under the eminent Professor Shaler. Darsie's parents, however, had hoped he would go to the University of Oregon. He was one of the first people to answer an ad our family had placed in the newspaper for a tutor in mathematics for my younger brother, Jim, who had just entered Yale at a very young age. I interviewed this big, handsome man, a member of the Harvard crew. He got the job. Besides which, when he returned to his room, he told his roommate he had just met the girl he wanted to be his wife."

Another time when I visited Sydney on a Saturday, she was holding a football chart in front of her while listening to a radio broadcast of a University of Washington football game. Each time a play was made, she recorded it on her chart. She was having a wonderful time by herself, rooting for the University of Washington team. While she was recording the game, I noticed some beautiful paper dolls lying on a table in the room that had obviously been done by hand in pastels. Just as I surmised, Sydney had made them for her granddaughters. She told me that when she was thirteen, Jim was sick with a fever, and dreamed strange dreams of weird animals. After he described them to her, Sydney sketched them — leopards with warts instead of spots and elephants with big fringes on their backs. Not only her brother was delighted with the drawings. A well-known artist, Eric Pape, happened to see her work amd recognized a great talent. Later on she was motivated to attend art school, specializing in fashion design. But when she met Darsie, she left all this behind.

A year's engagement led to a quiet marriage, an elopement of sorts, to avoid a big family wedding. Immediately after the wedding Darsie left for Butte, Montana, the great mining metropolis of that period. As soon as he found a place to work and live, he sent for Sydney. From that time on, Sydney's life with Darsie consisted of a series of moves. Darsie's work took him many places, and Sydney was always ready to pick up and follow, even when the babies were small. When they had two babies, they moved to Mexico, where one of the many adjustments they had to make was getting used to the frequent earthquakes. Later they lived in Idaho, and finally ended up in Seattle where in time they moved to the Victorian house in Laurelhurst.

Sydney loved her life in Seattle, with her four children and another on the way. But one Sunday afternoon all was changed. The children were busy on various projects, and Sydney herself was painting, when a telegram came: Darsie had come down with pneumonia. Could Sydney come at once? In those days they didn't have great medical expertise in treating this disease, and within days Darsie died.

Mary once told me about that sad time. "Sydney was devastated and we children were bewildered, not realizing how our lives would change, but totally aware that something was tragically wrong. One morning Sydney refused to get up and face the world. I went to her bedside and pleaded with her. 'The rest of us need you — you've just got to get up and carry on.' And Sydney certainly did."

A few weeks before Jill Ann Hutchings was born, I made my usual drop-in visit to Sydney's. The day before I had run into my brother, Ralph, at Mother's. It was the first time he had seen his little sister pregnant. He greeted me with, "Oh Lord, a short woman should never get pregnant — you look like a bloated Humpty Dumpty." And I felt just like that when I sank down beside Sydney on her sofa. I told her what Ralph had said and she answered, "When I was having my babies, I made myself a hammock-like arrangement with straps over the shoulders. I used it especially during the last stages of pregnancy. If you bring me two yards of heavy unbleached muslin, I'll make one for you."

I returned the next day with the material. The finished product had tabs that tied around my extensive girth. Little darts up the front made a strong nest for my stomach. The straps over the shoulders carried some of the weight. It made a big difference. Sydney should have patented her effective garment.

I continued my walks down to Sydney's after Jill was born, pushing her in a large, gray wicker perambulator. Those visits were productive. Sydney always gave me good parenting advice and the baby received great adoration. When Jill started to talk at an early age, Sydney told me that all of her children talked very early — all but Betty. She kept wondering when

Betty would start because she had shown great intelligence in every other possible way. Finally when she did start, she spoke in complete sentences with every word pronounced exactly right. I thought, *How like Betty to sit back, get the situation completely in hand, and then come forth with just the right words.*

CHAPTER 14

San Francisco or The Pines

$\mathcal{N}$ow that I was completely engrossed in being a wife, mother, and housekeeper, my world was a bit different from Betty's and we rarely saw each other. In my visits with Sydney, however, I kept abreast of Betty's activities. Besides being the first female labor inspector in the United States, working for the National Recovery Administration, she was having a good time socially.

Although I loved taking care of my blue-eyed, curly-haired, bright baby girl, the daily formulas to be made, the interminable washings — to say nothing of the housecleaning to keep up with Anne's standards — made me consider my life sheer drudgery. When Jill was just past her first birthday, Jock came home one evening with a wonderful invitation. We had both been invited by his insurance company to go to a conference in San Francisco. He had been to many before without me, so for me to be invited also was a great bonus.

We were to stay at the Sir Francis Drake Hotel which was fairly new. Jock had stayed there before and had told me once about a particular waitress in the coffee shop who made a specialty of opening a three-minute boiled egg with great aplomb and efficiency. It was a minor thing, yet it intrigued me that a gimmick like that could attract people from near and far to that one particular coffee shop. Of course, there were other more flashy reasons for being thrilled about going to San Francisco.

Jock said we would be going out every night — dining and

dancing, nightclubbing, and, no doubt, visiting the Barbary Coast dives. What a delightful change from my usual routine! Anne said we would be visiting the fleshpots of an evil city, and that I should take good care of her son. To me, San Francisco had always represented the epitome of sophistication, and had the most cosmopolitan people in the world. I could hardly wait to get there.

Mother made me a new dress which I designed myself. It was a long, purple lace sheath, with splits up each side to make it comfortable for dancing. A bright cerise, floppy, silk flower accented the waistline, and I had pumps dyed to match. Those two colors together always sent me, and when I paraded in front of the long mirror, Mother quoted from *Ecclesiastes*: "Vanity of vanities; all is vanity."

When Jock and I danced together at the St. Francis Hotel to Ted Fiorito's big-name band playing "My Little Grass Shack in Kealakekua, Hawaii," I thought I was dancing on the moon. To this day, I consider that evening one of the high points of my life! Jock was so enchanting at a party that I forgot all our trivial tiffs over who carried out the garbage last, and forgave his staying out too late too many times with the boys and spending the money we had saved for the electric refrigerator on a second camel's hair coat for himself.

We lunched at the Palace Hotel with Jock's insurance friends. We danced at the Mark Hopkins Hotel to Anson Week's big-name band. The theme of this band was "Dancin' with Anson." After the dance we were taken to a speakeasy in a remote part of San Francisco. It was located above a garage. To get there we walked down a cold, damp, cement-lined hallway, stepped into an inconspicuous elevator, and pushed a button.

After a short ride up, the door opened onto an expansive club-like room with burgundy wall-to-wall carpeting. Soft, rosy-glow lights revealed numerous overstuffed sofas, chairs, and low tables. Formally dressed waiters, with their trays of drinks held high above their heads, wove in and out of the tables, serving the many customers. For a few minutes I had an extraterrestrial feeling and thought, *Gee, I am now leading the sophisticated San Francisco life that I always thought so desirable,* but when I saw all the money changing hands, I was suddenly jerked back into reality. It was time to chop off this fancy living and head back to Seattle where life was real.

In no time we were back. Jock was reporting to his office in the Exchange Building and I was on my hands and knees scrubbing the linoleum, getting ready for Anne to visit and hear about our trip. I had just verified my suspicions that the money I had accumulated for that much-wanted refrigerator had disappeared again, no doubt going for the nightclubbing we had done in San Francisco.

Shortly after our return, I phoned Betty. Sydney answered the phone, and when she heard my voice, said, "I have some distressing news for you." She told me Betty had been coughing a lot and was tired all the time. When the doctor examined her, he had recommended that she immediately enter the tuberculosis hospital.

Sadly, I hung up the phone and thought about the last time I had seen Betty. We had had fun as always, but she had mentioned how tired she was all the time. She was unusually thin also, but I thought that was by choice as she had often complained about being too fat.

Sydney had said, "Why not wait awhile before you visit her?" and I held out for one month. On the way to Firlands, which was north of Seattle proper and which Betty refers to in her book *The Plague and I* as "The Pines," I went over the various events Jock and I had experienced in San Francisco, but it occurred to me that perhaps I shouldn't tell about them since Betty was not circulating now. I would wait and see how things were at the hospital.

As the nurse showed me to Betty's area, we could hear

laughing and talking. The nurse laughed too. "Listen to Betty. She keeps us all laughing with her witticisms. Most of her roommates love her, but one sensitive girl who was in the same room had to be moved because she could not take Betty's humor. A super-sensitive person just doesn't understand her. Have a good visit, but please don't stay longer than a half-hour."

Betty introduced me as her old high-school chum and everyone started to talk at once. They had many little "in" jokes, favorite characters in the institution to laugh about, and anecdotes that made it seem as if life was semi-hilarious all the time. I just sat with my hands folded, my head turning from one girl to the other, listening to their happy chatter. Knowing that the next day I was going to be giving a dinner party for some of Jock's business friends who were in town, I had the urge to crawl into an empty bed and join in the fun.

When I looked at my watch, it was time to go. I patted Betty on the head and said my good-byes. "Well, Betty, you seem to be doing all right. Next time I come, maybe I'll tell you about our trip to San Francisco."

CHAPTER 15

Mike–A Swell Guy

$\mathcal{B}$ecause of Betty's upbeat attitude and wonderful sense of humor, her stay in the hospital was shorter than predicted. As she describes in *The Plague and I,* she went through quite an adjustment period when she returned home. When I recently re-read her story, I felt terrible that I hadn't been more sensitive to her feelings at that time, but the next thing I knew when I dropped in at her mother's to welcome her back into the real world, she was perched on the built-in bench in their breakfast nook, pounding away on an old L.C. Smith typewriter. Casually dressed in frayed white pants, a tattered white sweat shirt and tennis shoes spotted with gray paint, she was completely absorbed in her project.

"What are you typing?" Stacks of typewritten sheets covered the table.

"I'm writing about my experience at "The Pines," she said laughingly. "It's going to be a book!"

"Can you write a whole book about that?" I asked incredulously.

"Oh yes, I certainly can. The characters I met out there, I'll never forget. Sit down and I'll get you a cup of coffee."

As I sat, I looked down at the kitchen floor. It had been freshly painted but quite a few footprints tracked across its gray surface. "You've just painted that floor. Can you go in there yet?" I asked.

"Yes, we painted it this morning," Betty said nonchalantly, "but we've been in there several times already today. We painted it last weekend, too, and the same thing happened. This many people can't live in this house without going into the kitchen, so we'll probably try again next weekend, and even the next, if necessary. I guess our motto is 'If at first you don't succeed.'"

As we drank our coffee, Betty said, "I've got to tell you about my new boyfriend. His name is Mike Gordon and I met him last week at a luncheon. He lives in Eastern Washington, and he is so generous. Already he has invited the whole family to several parties."

At Christmas time when I stopped by the Bards' to leave a gift for Sydney, I could barely step into the living room. There were so many presents under the tree, they spilled into the dining room and halfway up the stairs to the bedrooms. Betty waved her hand over all like a magic wand, and said, "Mike." Towering above the beautifully wrapped packages were two shiny bicycles for Anne and Joan.

Betty later wrote about Mike in the July 1949 issue of *Readers' Digest,* in an article entitled "The Most Unforgettable Character I've Met":

> I'm sure no woman ever enjoyed the attention of a more lovable or more unusual suitor than Mike Gordon. Instead of flowers or candy, Mike would send me such gifts as a side of beef; 24 boxes of apples; four dozen pairs of nylons (slightly irregular as to size and color); 288 cans of split-pea soup, six handmade Tyrolean sweaters all exactly alike and all wrong sizes, 200 ears of corn, a dozen hams, or 307 bars of scented soap.

In this article Betty goes on to tell that all of Mike's friends were either *very wealty and prrrrrrominent* or they were not his friends and were *damn appleknockers* (transient workers

Betty and Mike in Eastern Washington.

who came to harvest apples in Eastern Washington). In the front of my copy of *The Egg and I,* Betty wrote, *Dear Botchee, This is a copy I autographed during the flurry — I'm not trying to be prrrrrominent — but I am wealty — from your oldest school chum — Betty.*

One time I asked Betty, "Do you feel at all obligated for all Mike does? What does he expect from you?"

Betty's quick answer was, "All I have to do is reach down and pat him on the cheek and make him laugh a lot." Mike may have been at least a foot shorter than Betty, but he was one of the nicest men in her life.

CHAPTER 16

Finances and A Move

$\mathscr{I}$ mentioned to Anne and Ernest what a time we had been having trying to save for a refrigerator. Ernest asked, "How much do refrigerators cost?"

How well I knew — I had been looking at every ad. "Seventy dollars at least," I answered quickly.

"How much do you have saved?"

"Twenty dollars now, but I did have quite a bit more before some of it disappeared around the time of our trip to San Francisco." I gave him a meaningful look.

"I understand," he said. "Those San Francisco trips always cost more than one plans, don't they, Anne?" Ernest Hutchings had been an insurance man for many years and spoke from experience. "I'll tell you what — when you get thirty-five dollars saved, I'll treat you to the rest."

Jock pricked up his ears at the offer, whereas before he had been cool to the idea of a refrigerator. The fund began to grow faster than ever before. In two weeks we had the specified amount. We celebrated the day the new General Electric refrigerator arrived. It was one of those early models with a huge motor on top that purred like a kitten. (Forty years later I saw that old trusty appliance in a beach cabin we had once owned and long since sold. The present owners said the machine stood there all winter long, cold and idle, but when they returned each summer and plugged it in, it would take off as though it hadn't missed a moment.)

We invited Anne and Ernest to come for dinner and help us move out of the old icebox and into the new. Anne and I worked together like the "Gold Dust Twins," discarding, transferring, wiping up, and re-arranging, while Jock and his dad moved the old icebox to the back of the car and took it to the dump. We decided it would be no kindness to give it to anyone. Anne and I were never better friends than when it was time to fill the new ice trays with water and shove them into the right slots in the new machine.

Now that I had my refrigerator, I turned my thoughts to my next project: to save enough money for a down payment on a house. My parents had never paid one cent of rent in their lives and anyone who rented received a questioning look from Mother, usually followed by, "Oh, do they pay rent?" The question was loaded with inference: poor management, hand-to-mouth existence, instability and a will-o'-the-wisp lifestyle. When she discovered that the Hutchings were merely renting their beautiful brick home with a view, they fell several rungs down the economy ladder she had privately constructed.

Jock and I were getting along well in our marital journey in about every department but the budget. He was still a clotheshorse, but since I had always said I would marry a man who enjoyed dressing up, I never came down too strongly when the bills for men's clothing showed up every month. In fact I was so proud of his wardrobe that when I had my girl-friends to lunch, part of the entertainment was to take them into our bedroom to look in Jock's closet.

Once Betty and I counted well over forty outfits hanging in a neat row. After showing my friends Jock's suits, I always ran my thumb and forefinger down the crease on the left sleeve of each jacket so they all would hang in precision order like so many parentheses. Betty watched me perform my routine sleeve exercise before closing the door and asked, "Why do you do that?"

"The first time I showed the suits, one fell down, and I hung it back on the hanger a bit carelessly. One of the sleeves became askew, and when Jock went to hang up his clothes, he noticed it and inquired, 'Who has been messing with my clothes?'" Betty laughed. "He sounds like Father Bear asking who has been eating his porridge."

The next few times I saw Betty, she inquired, "Are you keeping Father Bear's creases smooth?" That was Betty, always remembering the funny quirks in people and everyday life, and having fun with them.

Whenever budget talks arose between Jock and me, I would borrow a quote from my mother (but without giving her credit): "When we learn to handle wisely what we have, we will be provided with more." Jock hated that little philosophy and would head me off eventually. "Now don't trot out that old wheeze about handling money wisely — I tell you, the only solution is for me to get a better-paying job."

Betty was with me the afternoon Jock phoned. "Hooray! I've just had an offer of a good job. I know how to do the work, I won't have to travel much, and I will make half again as much money as I do now."

"Wonderful!" I said. "Are you going to take it?"

"Well, it has a catch."

"What? Hurry and tell me what the catch is!" I pleaded.

"The job is in Portland, Oregon."

My delight turned quickly to dismay. "I've always thought Portland would be a dull place to live. It only has that little trickle called the Willamette River, and Mount Hood. We have Mount Rainier, which is much higher, plus two mountain ranges. And good old Green Lake and Lake Washington — but best of all, Puget Sound."

"We'll talk about it when I get home. In the meantime, think about it."

When I related the news to Betty, she said, "At least you

Ernest, Jill, Blanche, Joe-dog and Anne after the usual Sunday dinner

wouldn't have Anne breathing down your neck in Portland. Remember her regular Friday afternoon phone calls, and the weekly Sunday dinner syndrome?"

"Yeah, but leave my family — leave you?"

Betty said, "I just played bridge the other night with Flavia McEachern. She lives in Portland now and she likes it. She has two little girls, Elizabeth and Marsha, one a little older than Jill and the other a bit younger." I had known Flavia slightly at Roosevelt High School, but she was a sophomore when I was a senior, and in high-school days that gap was as wide as the Grand Canyon. But her two little girls sounded perfect for Jill. Already I had a contact, thanks to Betty once again.

When Jock came home, the first thing he mentioned was how we could break away painlessly from the Sunday dinners with Anne and Ernest, and that the Friday phone calls would certainly fade out. Every Friday after Jock had spent part or all of the week traveling, Anne would phone around five-thirty and whine in a pathetic voice, "Has Son come in yet?" If he had been home for an hour or so, I would cover up by saying, "Oh, he has just come in the door." If he hadn't arrived yet, Anne would say, "I am so worried about him — all that driving he has to do. Would you please have him phone the minute he comes in?"

In retrospect, I regret that I catered to her with my lying, but I always had a tendency to make everyone happy, even if it meant having to create an unreal world. I have often thought if I had only started out demanding the first position a wife is entitled to, life would have been quite different for both Jock and me.

Jock and I were soon in accord that the move would be good for us. I was aware that my mother was spoiling me by doing all the free baby-sitting, and by always being ready to stitch up an outfit. Jock realized he needed to get away from Seattle where his parents could not be so dominant in our lives.

Mary phoned to tell us good-bye and to let us know she was pregnant. She wanted to make sure she saw Jill before we left as Betty had told her about our two-year-old's political prowess. "For some strange reason," Mary said, "I have an inordinate interest in babies these days."

Betty had told her about the parlor trick which our neighbor, a political science professor, had taught Jill. He and his wife were also expecting a baby in the next couple of months, so he spent quite a bit of time studying ours.

Jill was talking very well by the age of two. Professor Nordyke recognized a potential student and taught her some current data. He would ask her, "Who is the dictator of Germany?" and she would quickly say "Hitler." Of course he had already taught her all the answers.

Next, he would ask her the name of the dictator of Italy. We all loved to watch her answer, as she would draw her lips together and push them up and out, almost touching her nose. "Mu-u-usssolini," she would say, with the *Mu* part drawn out.

The third question was, of course, "Who is the president of the United States?" Jill's voice was a little louder on this answer, drawing out the first syllable twice as long as the rest of the word. "Ro-oosevelt."

Professor Nordyke was proud of his success with this likely pupil. Jock and I were quick to latch onto this little trick and ask Jill to perform for any willing — or unwilling — listener. No matter how involved Jill was with a doll or teddy bear, she would stop her play and oblige.

A few days before our actual departure, I asked Mary and Jens to come for dessert, so we could formally say our farewells. When the evening arrived, Mary phoned to say Jens was involved in a case and they would be late. The dessert held up, but Jill didn't; she fell asleep on the floor and we had to put her to bed. Mary and Jens arrived over an hour late full of apologies. After we had our dessert and coffee, Mary said, "I'm sick about missing the performance. Now you are moving and we probably won't get to Portland until Jill is graduating from high school and delivering a valedictory."

Mary's plea was all the persuasion we vulnerable parents needed. Jock and I decided to wake Jill up to perform. We realized we were taking a chance, but we carried her into the living room, sleepy-eyed and swathed in a blanket. If Dr. Spock had been holding sway in those days, I am certain he would have written a paragraph about the dangers of selfish, egotistical parents exploiting their babies. But Jill didn't let us down. She answered each question with her eyes half-closed, but with full facial expressions. Jock and I poked her back into bed while basking in the praise of our guests. Mary's parting words were, "We have seen with our own eyes and heard with our own ears the two-year-old political scientist. Now Godspeed you and Jock to Portland."

CHAPTER 17

Portland–No Betty or Mary to Brighten My Life

*J*ock stayed at the Roosevelt Hotel in Portland while orient-ing himself to his new job and looking for a house for us to rent. When he thought he had found a suitable one, I flew down to look it over while Anne happily looked after Jill.

The house he had found was all right, but just around the corner was a wonderful Cape Cod in the last stages of con-struction. At first glance, I knew it was my dream house, the house for which I had been braiding a wool rug for four years. Painted white, it had two dormer windows upstairs and a bay window in the lower front, looking into the living room. Every room in the house was light and cheerful. There was a yellow-and-white bedroom for Jill, a blue-and-white one for the boy we hoped to have someday, and a large master bedroom in cream and beige tones. The lot was level with an interesting slope toward the sidewalk. But alas! It was not for rent — it was for sale. "Jock, we have $3.57 in our buy-a-house fund. How much more would we need to add to that for a down payment?"

"About nine hundred and ninety-six bucks." Jock prided himself on his rapid calculation.

"You'll be making more now, and we can use the addi-tional money for making the monthly payments. It's exactly the house I've always wanted — it has the perfect dining room for the rug I'm braiding."

Jock began to rally, "Look, we could put that white picket

fence you always talk about right along the sidewalk. This house screams for a picket fence."

"And Shasta daisies could be planted alongside it," I added.

"Three white birches could go there," Jock said, pointing to the top of the slope. We walked to the back of the house. "Hollyhocks would be perfect in front of the laurel hedge." I dreamed on.

Jock was cooperating nicely. "A sandbox for the kids could go here, and this nice level yard is perfect for croquet."

We had it all planned but the money. Jock said, "Let's describe it to Dad, and when his eyes begin to shine with interest, we can ask him for a thousand bucks."

"That should be a cinch for him, since he spent ten thousand dollars on your first year at Michigan," I said. "Did that include the raccoon coat and the Ford roadster? I've always wondered." (My first year at the University cost way under a thousand dollars.)

Whenever Jock was in a more playful mood, he would refer to himself as the "pampered son of a pauper." Though his father was not poor, he was comfortably well-off, and Jock's first year in college must have been spent like that of a son of a rich man — I didn't know anyone else who could afford to wear a raccoon coat. But they were very stylish!

Both Anne and Ernest loved our description of the house and they began to look not only interested but enthusiastic. Our plan had worked. They loaned us the needed money. Besides the monthly payment on the contract, we were to pay Ernest thirty-five dollars a month, interest-free. It was easy to tell Ernest he was an angel. In three weeks we were totally moved out of Seattle and into the Portland house, Jock's new company having paid the moving charges. Getting the house settled took a lot of my time, while Jock zeroed in on his new job.

Living in Portland away from our families was a first for me. We knew a few people who had already moved there from

Seattle, but most of the people we were seeing socially were new friends. I joined a preschool group and a sewing club, and, all too often, was invited to bridge parties. To please Jock, I took a few lessons in bridge and became proficient at quoting the rules, but I fell short as a partner when it came to remembering how many trumps were out and conjecturing who had the queen that might take my jack.

I enjoyed the preschool group the most because I was pregnant again and any current information on childrearing was meaningful. The sewing group gave me a good excuse to sit and knit, which I loved to do, but the conversations centered mostly on housework, such as which was the best wax for the kitchen linoleum, and how often the job should be done — not my favorite subjects.

Once there was a heated debate over whether you should have your hired girl sweep the kitchen before or after doing the dishes. The group who opted for sweeping first claimed that you walked the crumbs and spilled food into the floor if you waited, and the opposing group said that you should sweep the kitchen the very last thing before you left it, as there would be various spills to clean from dishwashing. I thought of the Lilliputians in *Gulliver's Travels,* one faction declaring war on the other because they broke their eggs on the large end while the others insisted on breaking them on the small. The Lilliputians fought for thirty-six moons before they finally settled the problem, but our sewing group spent over an hour discussing the pros and cons of sweeping sooner rather than later and finally left the debate open-ended.

At these women's sessions my mind would inadvertently roam to Betty and Mary; they would have had no time for such uninteresting discussions. And I thought of Sydney's suggestion that I ask the other women about books or gardening, but stay off the issue of housekeeping.

Our son was born exactly three years and four months

after Jill. We named him Keith Hamilton Hutchings. Keith was Jock's real name. When Jock first attended the University of Michigan, he went golfing with the Zeta Psis while being rushed. Jock's golf game left much to be desired. At that time there was a famous golfer by the name of Jock Hutchinson, and because Keith's efforts were so unproductive, his fraternity friends dubbed him Jock. The name stuck.

Baby Keith fit the description of a "bouncing baby boy" more than any other baby I had ever known. He was a real butterball who loved his bottle, and later, his vegetables and fruit. Most of the mothers of that era swore by the *Government Bulletin on Child Rearing*. One of the things advocated in that trusty pamphlet was to feed egg yolks to the baby, but not the whites (of course, this is now considered taboo). In order not to waste the whites, we mothers made many angel food cakes. I made so many angel food cakes that Jock offered to give me a dollar for every one I resisted baking. One month I resisted twenty times. It was the easiest money I ever earned.

One of the goals recommended by the *Bulletin* was to eliminate two of the every-four-hour feedings: the ones at twelve o'clock midnight and four a.m. But our baby loved to eat so much, it was a long time before we could get him to give up those two feedings willingly.

Our sleep was interrupted for months. We were invited out to play bridge with a couple upon whom Jock was anxious to make a good impression. They had no children. Much to Jock's chagrin, I went to sleep after making each play. He would have to nudge me awake and tell me it was my turn. Consequently, my performance was anything but dazzling and we were never again invited to play bridge with this special couple.

Jock joined the Aero Club, a social club recommended by his company as an appropriate place to entertain their clients. This meant we could eat there, attend their parties, and use the swimming pool. It sounded wonderful at first. The chief joy at the Aero Club was the pool, and as the children got bigger, we used it a great deal.

But eventually, I grew to hate the Aero Club because the bills kept getting larger and larger. In my opinion, Jock was too generous about buying drinks for anyone standing near the bar. Sometimes I would have dinner all ready and I would get a phone call that Joe from Pendleton was in town, and that he and Jock were going to stop by the Club for a drink. This often resulted in Jock's very late arrival home. The dinner would go untouched. I was not happy about those times.

Now we had our dream house with the braided rug spread tastefully on the dining room floor, the drop leaf maple table and ladder-back chairs, the picket fence with Shasta daisies peeking through the slats and three birches growing taller every day, and two adorable children. But there was something lacking. Being a housewife and mother, combined with the continual struggle to balance the budget, was not the perfect life for me. I did not have the answer. I missed my chats with Sydney and Betty and Mary, who, I am sure, could have put me on track. However, the events of the times changed everything, not only for us but for the whole world: Pearl Harbor was bombed by Japan on December 7, 1941.

At the time we had a Japanese girl living with us. She went to sewing school in the mornings and helped run the household the rest of the time. Her name was Sumi Furukawa. Jock begun to travel quite a bit for his company and I wanted to have someone with me, especially when he was gone. I put an ad in the newspaper. The wife of the minister of the church Sumi attended did the phoning for her. After the lady convinced me what a fine person Sumi was and I asked for an interview, she said, "By the way, the girl is Japanese. Does that make a difference?" It didn't matter to either Jock or me, so Sumi came out on the trolley to see if we would like each other.

She was charming, friendly, and giggled a lot. She had not

been in this country very long and her English was halting, but good enough for communication between us. I showed her to the room we had fixed for her with organdy curtains, a four-poster bed, and a warm rug on the floor. She liked the room but said she would not be able to sleep with her head toward the West, as Japanese people liked to have their heads toward the rising sun. When I said we could change it, she giggled and said, "No, I guess I don't really mind."

Sumi and I became good friends immediately. She was eager to do things "the American way" and took directions well. When I showed her how to make a pie crust, the first one she made was better than mine. It was amazing to me the way her crust stretched neatly over the fruit in the pie, with no patching.

Sumi had a boyfriend, Shiro Yonemura, who worked on a vegetable farm just outside Portland. He came to see her now and then, and sometimes they would visit by telephone. He was usually her only caller.

One rainy Sunday in December, however, while I was looking at the paper and listening to the radio at the same time, a car drove up and stopped in front of our house. The young man who got out of the car was Japanese, but not Shiro, who dressed casually and came on foot. This man wore a three-piece suit and carried a nice-looking briefcase. He knocked on the door and asked for Sumi, telling me that a mutual friend of theirs was a valet for Charlie Chaplin in Hollywood. He had been to visit this friend and wanted to show Sumi the snapshots he had taken.

I ushered him to Sumi's room. She was surprised and delighted to see him. I went back to my paper and the radio program. Less than an hour after, I heard over the radio, "The Japanese bombed Pearl Harbor early this morning!" I couldn't believe my ears when the distressing details followed.

Cold chills crept up my back. Here I was with a strange Japanese man in the house and Jock was away on a business trip. How did I know there were really snapshots of Charlie Chaplin in that leather briefcase? Maybe he was carrying a bomb! My reaction was purely emotional — certainly not cerebral — but typical of many people who were caught up in the anti-Japanese hysteria that began then.

I walked reluctantly down the hall, hesitating in front of the door. I could hear Sumi and her friend laughing and talking in Japanese. Should I knock and tell them what I had heard? It occurred to me that they would soon know, so I knocked. Sumi came to the door. Pictures were spread out over her desk, as her friend had visited California for two weeks.

"Have you had the radio on?" I asked.

"No, we have been looking at his pictures. He has been to Hollywood," Sumi said excitedly.

"I just heard over the radio that Japan has bombed Pearl Harbor in Hawaii," I stated bluntly. I'll never forget the stunned expression on their faces. Perhaps it was brutal of me to interrupt their pleasure that way. They looked at each other and went pale.

"What will that mean?" asked Sumi.

Her friend immediately started picking up his pictures. All he said was, "I'll see you soon — good-bye, Sumi," and he hurried out the door.

Sumi followed me to the living room. We stood staring at each other in bewilderment. I put my arm around her and said, "No matter what, Sumi, we are friends, aren't we?" I really liked her, and sensed what a turmoil her mind must have been in. Neither of us could possibly realize what the future held.

Life at our house went on as usual for a while, but when Jock came home from his trip to Eastern Oregon, he said, "I'm going to join the Air Corps. They're taking men like me. Several guys I saw in Pendleton say they're going to join up, too." I thought it was just talk, but soon I realized he meant every word.

Our neighbor, Mrs. Bray, who sold Avon products, came by one day to deliver my order. I asked her to sit down a minute before she started the walk back up the long hill to her home.

"Have you heard from Jack?" Her son was in the Navy, serving in the Pacific somewhere.

"No, I haven't, not for three weeks, and I am really worried," she answered. As we were talking, the telephone rang. Sumi answered and began speaking rapidly in Japanese as she always did when the caller was Shiro.

Mrs. Bray scowled at me angrily. "Are you going to continue to allow that girl to live in your home? I wouldn't have her another minute."

"We are friends," I answered. "She knew nothing about Pearl Harbor until I told her."

Mrs. Bray left the house hurriedly, looking back at me unhappily over her shoulder. I am sure she thought I was harboring a spy.

Shiro was sent to an internment camp soon after that. While there, he often phoned and asked Sumi to bring him certain items when she visited. In another month, she packed up her things and joined him. They were moved from Portland to Idaho, both to the same camp. In a short time they were married in Spokane, Washington. When the war was over and they were released to rejoin the world, they moved to a large vegetable farm in Oregon owned by Sumi's brother. There they have lived and raised a family of four children, three girls and a boy, who have all have done very well in our western culture. Through the years, we have kept in touch with each other via Christmas messages.

For myself in those troubled times, I began to plan where the children and I should live after Jock joined the service. My thoughts turned northward, back to Seattle and Puget Sound.

PART

3

CHAPTER 18

The Galapagos and Vashon Islands

The friends we had made in Portland were all fine people, but I missed my regular contact with the Bards. On my frequent visits to Seattle I always dropped in to see Sydney, show her the kids, and hear about Mary and Betty. Mary was busy with her young daughters and Betty was dating interesting men. Mike was still holding his own and providing glamorous ways of entertaining not only Betty, but anyone else in the family she would like to include.

Since Jock meant what he said about joining up, I was turning over various ideas about what to do with my life. I knew definitely I would not stay in Portland where I had fallen into a syndrome of keeping up with the Joneses. I knew better but felt I was trapped. In this neighborhood, in order to be accepted you had to have the right cleaning woman and beauty operator, and make sure not to wear a straw hat when the month of September rolled around. A style-minded friend of mine refused to sit with me at a P.T.A. meeting because I came with a neighbor who was still wearing her navy straw hat — and it was already September 17.

I had a roommate in college who lived in the town of Burton on Vashon, an island situated between Seattle and Tacoma in Puget Sound. Her father, a semi-retired dentist, had installed a dentist chair and the minimum of trappings that go with the skill in a room over the Harbor Mercantile General Store. He took patients three times a week and accommodated emergencies at any hour of day or night. Irene entertained me endlessly with stories of the interesting characters in Burton.

When I visited Irene, she took me to meet a wealthy jeweler's wife from Chicago, Mrs. Banger. Mrs. Banger had fallen in love with the area known as Quartermaster, and built herself a little hideaway on the isthmus of the peninsula that separates Inner from Outer Quartermaster. A personal friend of Havelock Ellis, she had many signed photographs of him hanging on her walls. Her beautiful grand piano sat on a dais which also served as a stage for her daughters, who spent summers with her and put on little plays. Irene told me in confidence that Mrs. Banger often walked around in the nude because it made her feel so free, and because it was something she couldn't do very well in Chicago. I was intrigued with such an avant garde lifestyle.

Then we met Granny Higgins as we went to the village post office to pick up the mail. Granny had always wanted a fireplace and could not afford one. Rather than do without, she asked an artistic friend to paint one on the wall, complete with a glowing log fire. She would pull her rocking chair up to the wall, have a cup of tea and become toasty warm. Granny always wore a long, full, dark skirt. Sometimes when she returned from picking up her mail, she would stop a minute or two at the roadside, supposedly to glance at a letter. When she moved on, there would be a little puddle where she had stood. Her underwear, like many our great grandmothers wore, had a big slit in the crotch, designed for easy relief.

Irene's own family was warm, individualistic, and expert at getting fun and joy out of the tiny aspects of living. Her mother, for example, went into ecstacies over the treasures she found in the flotsam and jetsam at high tide.

Burton was tucked away in the back of my mind as the place to flee to when city living became oppressive. Now that Jock was definite about joining the Air Corps, my thoughts

Jock Hutchings joined the United States Air Corps in 1942.

latched onto Burton. That was the place for me. Maybe I could become one of those interesting characters in that little village. And moving there meant we would be closer to our families again. Since Jock was doing what he wanted, he was willing to let me do what I wanted.

Anne and Ernest were plainly upset about the whole thing. While we were cutting up carrots for a vegetable soup, Anne said, "Daddy and I have talked this over and we have decided that you and the children can move in with us. I don't want to see Son go, but believe me, I am not going to let my friends know that. I am going to say to them, 'Jock is joining the Air Corps. He is going with our blessing because he is doing the patriotic thing that all other American men should be doing. He is serving Old Glory!' She lifted her chest and held her head high. We should have finalized the scene by saluting the American flag, but I didn't keep one in the kitchen. Secretly I felt that Jock was looking for adventure while wrapping himself in the flag.

Events began to turn fast. Our little white dream house went up for sale. I took a hurried trip to Vashon Island and in less than a day, found an appealing piece of property facing the Outer Harbor. The three-quarter acre included two beach cabins fronted by a low bank and a sandy beach with a bounty of butter clams that could be dug with a simple sharp stick if you couldn't find the shovel. There was a six-room house up on the bank with two big maple trees flanking either side of the path that led to the beach. On the roadside of the property sat a three-room cottage with a view of the Inner Harbor. A plumber was renting that place and I was advised by the seller to keep him on as the plumbing was very old in all the buildings.

All this property was available for only $3750. (But that was in 1940. In 1990, the cottage alone sold for $50,000.) Jock liked the place also, so we consummated the deal.

Anne and Ernest tried valiantly to be good sports about our move, and Ernest did a lot of tapping on walls, shaking his head and saying, "Not much insulation here. Come winter, you might have to move in with us." I changed the subject.

I was excited about the move, although the house was a far cry from my Cape Cod dream house. When the movers arrived with our furniture, one of the brawny fellows actually wrinkled his nose when he got out of the truck. "You folks movin' here after that classy house in Portland?"

But everybody in our family was happy about what we were doing. The children, now four and seven years old, were looking forward to life on a salt water beach. Jill would be entering the third grade at a charming little school located near a wooded area on the Inner Harbor. Keith would have his own beach and Jock would hang a big rope swing on the lower branch of one of the maple trees. For me, there would be a hammock swung between two transparent apple trees. And we could get another dog, a playmate for our dachshund, Gretchen.

It took time for Jock to get his papers ranking him as a First Lieutenant. Finally the orders came for him to ship out to the Galapagos Islands. He had ambivalent feelings about this assignment — it would offer adventure but not much chance to win a Purple Heart. I was relieved.

So was Anne, who now went by the name of Grommy. Not wanting the handle *Grandma* or *Grandmother,* she whipped up Grommy instead, claiming it was a name contrived from

Mrs. E. M. Hutch-ings, "Grommy" to the kids. Jill is with her on a Seattle shopping trip.

Jill's baby talk. I stood idly by and watched the name evolve — not from the kids, but from Grommy herself. Anne thought the name had a dramatic overtone that made her stand apart. It did. At about the same time, Ernest became Pampy but this was a legitimate invention of Keith's. I thought the name had a sweet, warm, grandpappy sound to it. Ernest deserved a good name.

As soon as Jock's papers were in order and plans were actually materializing for his leavetaking, Grommy quickly came up with a plan. She and Pampy would take Son to the train by driving from Seattle to our house to pick him up, take the ferry at Tahlequah to Pt. Defiance, and then drive him to the train depot in Tacoma. Son would say his final goodbyes to the children and me at home.

I knew the departure from Tacoma would be as dramatic as Anne could make it — with much hugging and kissing, a stiff upper lip until the train pulled out, and then buckets of tears. I agreed to her plan in order to be spared some of the histrionics, but Esther pointed out when she heard the plan that I, as Jock's wife, should have taken him to the train while Pampy and Grommy baby-sat the kids. In retrospect I agreed with my sister, but that little episode epitomized the family situation. Anne had never released her son to a wife, nor did I ever pitch battle to capture my wifely roll. As my mother so aptly put it, quoting again from another old adage: "A daughter is a daughter all her life, but a son is a son till he takes a wife." And then Mother added coyly, "I guess Anne has never heard that."

CHAPTER 19

Surprises–Old Friends

$\mathcal{A}$s soon as Jock was gone, an easy friendship developed between Ann and me. We had lunch together at Frederick and Nelson's tearoom, which at that time was the "right" place to go. Each time we met, Anne would buy me a blouse, a dress, or some cute little trinket. On some weekends the children and I rode the ferry over to Seattle to spend time with Anne and Ernest. Keith loved Pampy's spotless workshop in his basement. All his tools hung on the wall with lines drawn around each one, so that whenever one was taken down, it could be replaced speedily. Pampy helped Keith make little boats and animals with his coping saw. Their relationship was a precious one.

Life was not at all dull for me. My first job was to lay new linoleum in the kitchen. It sounded simple. I thought all it entailed was choosing the linoleum and paying for it, after which the man would deliver and install it. Little did I realize that my kitchen range had coils to heat the water in the tank, and that I needed a plumber to disconnect the pipes so the stove could be moved out of the way. Another helpful revelation at the time was that a person needed to coordinate her workers. The linoleum man arrived before the plumber, but we could do nothing until the stove was moved. I ran down to get my renter, but he and one of his pals were sitting at his breakfast table too far into their cups to listen to me. I tried to communicate with him, but with all the arm waving and sloppy enunciation, I knew a lost cause when I saw it.

I ran back to the linoleum man and in a tragic voice, explained the situation. "Well, lady, I do linoleums, that's my reg'lar work," he said, "but in a real emergency like this, I can disconnect them pipes. In fact, I carry a pipe wrench just in case." And he shuffled off to his truck to get it, muttering, "You know I got customers awaitin' fer me and I ain't got time to sit around waitin' for some drunk to come."

I was so thrilled when I saw the stove get pushed out and the new linoleum put in place that I didn't care a bit about the mess of water and ashes that lay all about the kitchen. When the job was finished, the linoleum man pulled out of the driveway just in time for the truck carrying the new stove to pull in. Pampy had told me that as the old stove was rusty and no good, he would buy us a new one. He said it was for my birthday, soon due. Much to my joy, the man delivering the new stove said installation was all part of the deal. Not only that, he worked with efficiency. I was almost ready to ask him to join me in a polka, I was so pleased with the way the project was falling into place.

The kids and I loved our kitchen with all the new things — such a contrast to the old stuff that had been there before. But, one evening about a month later, we had the table all set for dinner, when drip, drip, drip — water was rhythmically running down from somewhere, splattering on a dinner plate. I thought maybe someone had left the water running in the washbowl in the upstairs bathroom. I ran upstairs and saw the vulnerable spot, which looked like a poor connection in the pipes. Outside, rain was coming down in sheets, but I grabbed a newspaper to cover my head and ran for the plumber. This time he was stretched out on his kitchen floor with his pal, Buck, bending over him, trying ineffectively to get him to drink some black coffee.

I stood in the doorway and blurted out my pipe problem to Buck. Then I added, "I'm really in need of someone right away." My patience with the plumber was running low. He was out! Buck was still sober enough to see that my situation needed instant attention. He pulled himself together and said, "Well, Ed and I were jist a havin' a few little drinks and his hit him pretty hard. I was tryin' to get him to drink a little coffee. I can see you're in trouble, tryin' to get dinner an' all. I can fix that for yuh, Missus; I'll be right up as soon as I find Ed's tools."

It seemed an hour before Buck arrived but I had already put a washpan on the table to catch the water. He knew where the shut-off was as he had pinch-hit for Buck before. He proceeded to do the necessary. After thirty minutes he left the house with much gallantry, shaking my hand and telling me to never mind the bill — the job was on him because his pal was "a little under the weather," as he put it.

We finally got the water wiped up and sat down to our meal. I was almost too tired to eat but saw that the kids were in their places at the table looking expectant of food, so I flopped into my chair. Mother, who had come to visit for a few days, had gone into the other room. I called her to the table. When she arrived, she was carrying gifts on a tray and singing "Happy Birthday to You." The children joined in. The struggle for survival in our new abode had made me momentarily forget my birthday even though that was why Mother was visiting in the first place.

Even when the plumbing was working well, we never seemed to get enough hot water. It all depended on how much we used the kitchen range with the coils. Because of this difficulty we had to schedule our baths carefully, and when we all needed one, we chose the cleanest person to take the first one. It was fun to see how the children would try to prove to me how clean they were by pulling down socks or shoving up sleeves. Many times we had to draw straws to settle the choice. Once a month Gretchen got the last bath. She caught on to our schedule and hid under my bed when it was her turn. The only guarantee for getting her bathed was to tie her up when the first person stepped into the tub. I took dips in Quartermaster waters every morning except when there was snow on the ground. This custom not only made me feel clean but got my blood circulating for the day's ever-occurring challenges.

To compensate for the tricky plumbing, our living room was cheerful, with five sets of double, old-fashioned, pull-up-and-down windows at which I hung white dotted Swiss curtains. A friend of my dad's cut the front door in half, making an attractive Dutch door that opened out onto an expansive front veranda. The baby grand piano fitted nicely under the winding staircase that led from the living room up to our bedrooms. And yes, my masterpiece, the hand-braided rug, fit perfectly in our dining room. Just as I had everything fairly well-organized and was planning to do some "hammock reading" under the apple trees, a couple came strolling up the long path to the house from the beach. I ran to the porch to see who it could be.

I thought at first they were trespassers, but they turned out to be old friends, Florrie and Johnny Robblee. I had gone to college with Florrie and had been in her wedding several years before. All three of us were very surprised to see each other. They wanted to rent a cabin. I threw up my hands in dismay, as the thought of another house project seemed overwhelming. They promised to do most of the work to get the cabin ready and before I knew it, I was agreeing to rent to them.

The cabin had one of those old-fashioned toilets with the tank mounted on the wall up behind the stool. You flushed by pulling a long chain. The first time I tried to flush that toilet, a huge pipefitting came crashing down on my head. I didn't mind the bump so much, but the thought of dealing with my plumber-renter again was depressing. I had honored the statement that this estate needed to have a plumber handy, but inexperience had prevented my insisting on a sober one. Ed was the first plumber I ever dealt with, and although it isn't fair, I've viewed all plumbers since with a jaundiced eye. Just say the word *plumber* and I conjure up a mental image of my renter stretched out on the floor.

However, this time I contacted him early in the morning and he even offered me a cup of coffee. The Robblees reported later that his job was very professional, and they used the antique toilet without incident the rest of the season. This good report almost restored my faith.

A week later, some friends of the Robblees came to visit and decided they wanted to rent the other cabin. My cabin business was growing despite the fact I didn't want it to. When Esther saw my set-up, she accused me of being a schemer. "I bet you send your kids to the beach and expect your renters to check on them while you loll in the hammock!"

When fall came to Burton, nature outdid herself in turning everything amber, orange, and gold. The maple trees that lined the water's edge doubled their splendor by reflecting in the smooth waters of Quartermaster. Innumerable Madrona trees, said to grow only in the Northwest, proudly displayed their smooth reddish-orange bark, which shone twice as brilliantly with the soft sidelighting of the autumn sun.

When Jill came home from school, the children, Gretchen and I took walks in the incredible stillness of our little village. We dragged our feet through the fallen maple leaves, loving the crisp, swishing sounds we generated. The acrid scent of fall clean-up fires permeated the air. Feelings of complete satisfaction swept over me on those walks. Life on the island was right for us. Not once was I sorry for the move, even though we had to live with temperamental plumbing.

My stipend from the government was two hundred dollars a month. Even in 1940 that was a skimpy income for three people, so I stopped by the School Superintendent's office and registered for substitute teaching. In a few days I received my first call, to take the place of a fifth-grade teacher who would be gone a week. I phoned Mother, now a widow, to come over and spend the week with us and keep Keith company.

It was exciting to get back into the schoolroom again. I boned up on the fifth-grade curriculum before I went. Mother was perfect as a babysitter, as she loved to read and Keith loved to be read to. One morning at Sunday School, when he was being taught about Moses and the Red Sea, he said to his teacher, "When we finish with Moses, let's do Heathcliffe." (Mother had become weary of *The Three Little Pigs*, and had launched into the book she was reading, *Wuthering Heights*.)

The teacher accommodated Keith, saying, "*You* tell us about him." She later told me that what he recounted was so interesting, she went to the library the next day and checked out the book.

At the end of the week I was asked to stay on, since the regular teacher had left in order to work at Boeing, where she could make more money. When I got paid for that week of teaching, my own check gave me a wonderful feeling of independence. I felt so good about having earned an extra twenty-five dollars that I invited Anne to lunch at Frederick's, to help me pick out a new dress to wear to the evening P.T.A. meeting at which I would be formally introduced to the other teachers and parents. A friend who had seen Anne and me laughing and talking together said, "I wish I could have as much fun with my mother-in-law as you seem to have with yours." It was a new relationship for the two of us because the "bone of contention" was in the Galapagos.

A month after my father died, Mother agreed to move in with me permanently and rent her house in Seattle. She stipulated, however, that I would have to guarantee to keep her warm. We put a circulating heater in the living room and removed the little airtight stove which was supposed to have been heating a six-room house. I knew I had better start laying in stove wood before winter was upon us. Friends told me it was going to be a tough job to get wood because so many of the wood men had gone to war. Tuck Miller had all the orders he could fill and absolutely would take no more, and his brother-in-law, Joe, had left for the battle zone the week before. Every time I heard a name connected with the word *wood*, I wrote it down. I made phone calls and wrote notes, playing up the fact that I had two small children and a mother in her late seventies to keep warm. Mother said, "You have done everything a human can do. Now I shall pray that we will be supplied with all the wood we need."

One day she phoned me at school. Excitedly she said, "Blanche, you had better cancel some of those wood orders right away. The third cord has just arrived and now you won't be able to get into your garage!" True enough, when I turned into our driveway after school, all I could see were stacks of wood and just the sloping roof of the house. The kids helped me move enough so I could barely maneuver the car into the garage. As I walked to the house, picking my way between chunks of wood, Mother met me at the door. "Daughter, our prayers have been answered and now our cup runneth over."

The next day at school, I walked into the girls' lavatory looking for a girl who had lost her lunch pail. There, standing before the mirror, combing her long, blond hair, stood a new student. I took a second look. "Joan, is that you?" She turned around and smiled. Yes, it was Joan MacDonald, Betty's younger daughter!

"How do you happen to be here?" I asked.

I got the answer I had hoped for. "We just moved here yesterday and Betty is making us start school right away. Anne is at the high school. How do *you* happen to be here?"

Neither Betty nor I knew the other was moving to Vashon. Now, once again, our paths were crossing. Betty had remarried

Betty MacDonald in the garden of her Vashon home. (Courtesy of the Seattle Times.)

and as she recounts in *Onions in the Stew,* she landed on Vashon Island. With a war on, many people moved to Seattle to work for Boeing and in the shipyards. Finding a house either to rent or buy was impossible. It was almost a miracle that Betty and her husband found their wonderful place on the island.

I quickly told Joan why we were here. "Be sure to tell your mom that we are now living in Burton. I am teaching the fifth grade here."

"We live at Dolphin Point at the north end of the island," Joan said. "We have a beautiful house on the beach, but we had to move our furniture in by rowboat. Betty's new husband is Don MacDonald, and he is very handsome." Joan rolled her pretty blue eyes.

CHAPTER 20

The Scheherazade Suite *or* "*Yes, We Have No Bananas*"

*W*hat a bonus to find Betty so close at hand! I hoped we could pick up our friendship where we had left off a few years back. But now she had a husband and I didn't, at least temporarily, which could make a difference. She didn't have a phone yet, so she sent a message via Joan inviting me to their house. I was eager to see her and hear about all the exciting things that had occurred in her life since the last time we talked. There had been no potential husband in sight when I had left Seattle for Portland.

The first time I visited Betty, it was pouring rain. I parked my car at the side of the main highway and eventually found the narrow path that led to her place. Ferns, milkweed, and plantain heavy with rainwater leaned over and licked at my ankles and legs all the way. When I arrived at her spectacular house, I was soaked to the knees. I knew that Betty and her family walked that trail at least twice a day without complaining, so I said not a word, but when Betty looked at my feet and legs, she said, "I thought you came by the path!"

"I did, but I'm soaking wet," I admitted.

"You look as though you had come by the beach at high tide! That is the way we moved in here, but we did have a row-boat." Her eyes twinkled. As there was no road into her place, you chose either the path or the beach, but if you came the latter way at high tide you needed a boat — or a wet suit.

Betty introduced me to her handsome husband, Don, "my

dour Scotsman," as she referred to him. He was tall and round of face, with dark curly hair cropped close to his head. Then she showed me around the house, which was rustic, very beachy-looking, with a large granite fireplace. Yellow pots of red geraniums stood on the windowsills in the cheerful kitchen, which was separated from the large living room by an eating area. A few steps led up to three bedrooms and a bathroom on the same level. The railings along this little balcony were thin, highly polished logs. These logs and the hand-hewn rafters on the high ceiling added to the rustic ambiance of the house. It was a dramatic place, but I was never quite warm enough when I visited.

During that first visit, our chatter began immediately as we had so much to tell each other, what with her recent marriage and the changes in our families brought on by the war. Eventually Betty wanted to know about the schools her two girls were attending.

Eminent in my mind was the loss of several teachers and a principal to the higher wages Boeing could afford to pay. One morning just the week before, I had dropped by the principal's classroom (he also taught eighth grade and performed all his duties from one desk) to get some keys. On his desk was an open, abrupt note: "Won't be back — gone to work at Boeing," after which he had signed his name. A substitute was hired until the school board could find a permanent replacement.

Sometime after our first reunion, Betty phoned to say she would be coming to the P.T.A. meeting as she wished to meet Joan's teacher and the principal. After I introduced them, Betty and I stepped into the meeting in the auditorium. Again, just as in high school, our sitting together was a big mistake. I knew it immediately. Betty's remarks were too funny for a staid P.T.A. meeting. Almost everyone there was dressed casually, which was the norm for Vashon Island. Cotton dresses with sweaters thrown over shoulders, light-colored pants, flowered and plaid blouses surrounded us. Had it been a few years later, everyone would have been wearing jeans.

All at once, the P.T.A. president swept into the room. For a minute I thought I was back in Portland at the Duniway School, where the monthly P.T.A. meeting was a seasonal style show. This president was petite, pretty, and dressed in a navy blue, raw silk suit. Her blouse was pale pink organdy with a ruffle at the neck that peeked out in the right places. Her large navy straw picture hat had a floppy rose at the right of center, where crown met brim. Her pink-and-white face looked incredibly sweet as she smiled over the ruffle. With a white-gloved hand, she picked up the silver-trimmed gavel and gave a slight tap to bring the meeting to order. Her outfit was so incongruous compared to everyone else's attire and the simplicity of the room that Betty and I both stifled a giggle.

Next came the flag salute led by Madam President herself, during which we had the opportunity to cover up our laughter and regain our composure. Later in the meeting the president made a flowery speech to present a gift to the hot-lunch cook. It was too much. Mrs. Hawkins, the cook, was a large, forthright woman who had been asked to leave the kitchen for a few minutes and step into the meeting. Still in her white overall apron, she strode into the room, looking puzzled as to why she had been summoned.

In her most unctuous voice, Madam President said, "It is indeed a privilege to present this token of our appreciation to our dear cook, Mrs. Hawkins. All this year she has been providing wonderful, nutritious meals for our children. I am sure she will receive many hours of enjoyment from these records of *The Scheherazade Suite*, by Rimsky-Korsakov."

As Mrs. Hawkins reached for her gift, she wrinkled her brow and asked, "The *what* suite?"

"*The Scheherazade Suite*, by Rimsky-Korsakov," repeated the president condescendingly.

"Oh sure, thanks a whole lot," said Mrs. Hawkins. She walked haltingly from the room, looking curiously at the artistically wrapped gift.

At this point, Betty whispered to me, "Everybody knows she'd rather have 'Yes, We Have No Bananas!'" Her remark was so apt, I started to laugh again. Then I saw my co-workers looking at Betty and me, and not too pleasantly. I needed to leave before I disgraced myself. I put my handkerchief to my nose and left the auditorium, hoping people would think I had a nosebleed.

My fellow teachers didn't know Betty. She was not famous yet. Thinking back, if they had been able to look into the future, they would have been more charitable toward me, sitting next to one of the wittiest women in the country. Betty was one of the few friends I ever had who not only enjoyed teasing, but liked being teased back even more.

One day I went into Seattle to pick up a secondhand car, and gave Betty a ride back to the island. Since the various instruments on the car were somewhat new to me, I said aloud, "Here is the turn signal, here is the clutch." I knew Betty didn't drive and wanted to lead her to believe I was more uninformed than I really was. First in line onto the car deck of the ferry, we were directed down the middle aisle. There was the gaping maw at the end of the boat, with Puget Sound beyond. Knowing full well I could stop when I had to, it was too tempting a moment not to tease.

"Oh gosh, Betty, I hope I can remember where the brake is, or else we'll go right off the end." Betty was giggling nervously, not knowing whether to believe me or not. My foot was ready for the brake and when I applied it, I said to her, "Yeah, that's it. Whew!"

"You knew all the time, didn't you?" She laughed and settled down easily in the seat.

The next week I was in the Vashon Hardware to replace a

plumber's helper that had been loaned and not returned. Mr. McCormick, the owner, waited on me. He put the article in a sack and handed it to me across the counter as I reached for my handbag. But I didn't have it. I said, "I am sorry, I must have left my handbag at school. Could I drop in tomorrow and pay for this then?"

Before he could answer, a voice from the store entrance said, "There's that deadbeat of a Mrs. Hutchins" — she left off the *g* in Hutchings to make it sound more plebeian — "trying to get out of paying for stuff again. Ha, saying she has forgotten her purse."

I knew the voice without looking. It was Betty, but there were other people in the store fixing their eyes on me. I looked at Mr. McCormick who had a twinkle in his eye. "I hope you have a sense of humor," I said. He smiled broadly.

As I walked out of the store, plumber's helper in hand, Betty called, "I've gotten even with you now for driving me off the ferry." People in the store looked curious as we laughed delightedly.

Sometime after that, when the rationing of coffee, sugar, and gasoline was necessary because of wartime shortages, the teachers were asked to serve on the rationing board. When Betty and Don arrived for their stamps, I was sitting at the table with several other volunteers. As they entered the room, I said, "Here come the MacDonalds. Watch them when they ask for their stamps — their basement shelves are sagging, they are so overloaded with the coffee they are hoarding."

Betty laughed self-consciously and everyone else laughed, too. I said, "Betty, remember the plumber's helper."

CHAPTER 21

In the Family

$\mathcal{O}$ften I would see Betty and Don on the ferry, which was always a lift. I think Betty felt the same way about me, but I am sure Don didn't. I would hurry towards them. Our tongues would start to waggle, usually about subjects in which Don held no interest. Sometimes he would excuse himself and go for a cup of coffee, or else head back to their car.

One time Betty was sitting between Don and her brother, Cleve, who was a tall, rugged, red-haired man. I always thought he looked like his father, from the pictures I had seen of Darsie. Cleve cut quite a figure on Vashon. He was very active in civic affairs and ran a successful construction business.

Betty invited me to sit down. "Listen to Cleve. He is trying to sell us his car, which is down on the car deck of this ferry. I want Don to go below to check it out, to be sure it has a motor. The last time we bought a car from Cleve, it only ran until we got home." Cleve took all this banter lightly as he understood his sister and her sense of humor.

Sydney spent a great deal of time with Betty, and I was impressed by what good friends they were. Sydney had such good advice about so many things, and Betty usually listened. In *Onions in the Stew*, Betty tells all about the trouble she had with pretty little Lesley Arnold, who was always trying to allure Don into her house, ostensibly to move a piece of furniture — after which she would offer him a drink. Lesley's husband was in the Navy and she was lonesome for a man's company.

One evening I was at the MacDonald's for dinner. It was getting later and later and Don hadn't arrived home. Betty was getting upset. "I know where he is — shall I call up down there?"

Sydney answered, "Betty, if I were you, I'd spend the time you'd take phoning to go and tidy up a bit. Put on clean pants, a fresh blouse, and smooth your hair. Undoubtedly Lesley needed another piece of furniture moved. She has probably put on one of her frilly, feminine frocks and is turning on her inimitable charm full bore. If Don comes home and finds you tired, mad, and sarcastic, the contrast will not be in your favor."

Betty followed her mother's suggestions. When Don strolled up the path, she was very cheerful, looked lovely, and did not mention how late he was.

Betty loved good food and she enjoyed cooking. That evening, as always, she had prepared an excellent meal but it had taken her hours. She had made a crust of flour, water, shortening, and salt. After rolling it out, she wrapped it around a beef roast which she already had seasoned, taking care to seal the roast entirely. Then she put the roast in the oven. When it was served, it was as succulent a piece of meat as I had ever eaten. The fluffy mashed potatoes with brown gravy and fresh peas made the plate not only delicious but eye-appealing as well. On the side was a salad of grapefuit slabs and avocado on crisp lettuce — Betty's favorite. The Bards were never ones for many sweets, and the final course was an interesting assortment of cheeses with grapes. Don complimented her on the fine meal and I felt sure Betty had won that evening's honors over the fluffy little Lesley.

You have only to read a line or two of Betty's writing to know that another one of her loves was words; her similes and metaphors were incredibly apt. The way people talked and used our language was important to her. Once while she was pressing one of her daughter's blouses, she found a note in the pocket. Betty unplugged the iron and walked over to show it to me. "Listen to this, Blanchie: 'Dear Anne, I am afraid you are taking me for granite.' What kind of a kid is this? She can't be overly bright," she grumbled.

I answered, probably not too comfortingly, "At least there are no four-letter words. Be grateful for that." (Those were the "good old days," when four-letter words were considered naughty.)

Another time we were talking about some offbeat people we knew who had rather peculiar sleeping arrangements within their family. Betty said, "Of course, they 'incested' everything was open and aboveboard."

Both Betty and Mary wrote and said witty things, but Betty quoted Mary to me much more often than the other way around. Mary's doctor-husband was in the Navy, but Mary did not sit still and pine. She engaged herself in many worthwhile causes and also did a lot of entertaining. Betty claimed that when Mary wanted to be the hostess par excellence, she brought her guests to Vashon, not always giving much prior notice.

Once when Mary was on her way over with several guests, the septic tank acted up and unpleasant substances were backing up in the pipes. When Mary and her guests swung merrily down the path into the garden area, Betty greeted them with, "I hope you will forgive us for using this moment to clean out our septic tank. We're in trouble."

Mary replied cheerfully, "Betty, you needn't apologize. It is the ultimate in hospitality for the hostess to clean out her septic tank when company is coming. We are all terribly flattered that you would go to all this trouble." And Mary and her friends went on into the house and made themselves comfortable in the living room.

Mary had many contacts about town. One time at a cocktail party, she met a representative from Doubleday Publishers. She happened to mention to him that her sister, Betty, was writing. The gentleman was particularly interested in Western authors. Mary told him a few stories about Betty's life on the Olympic Peninsula. To my knowledge Betty had not yet written about her experiences on the chicken farm but had only recounted them orally. The representative told Mary that he would like to see a written outline of Betty's experiences, and that if it could be delivered to him by five o'clock the next day, he would give her work serious consideration.

Mary rushed to the phone and relayed the message to Betty, who literally took her hands out of the dishwater and sat down to prepare the outline. She stayed up most of the night, getting it in order to present the next day. She made the deadline, although she did miss a day of work. The Doubleday representative was so pleased with the outline, he offered her five hundred dollars on the spot.

For some reason, sometime after Doubleday bought the outline, they sold it to Lippincott. What a happy day for Lippincott — that publisher had just bought what was to become a best seller. And Betty was launched on her way to success as a writer.

CHAPTER 22

Fame Brings Pain and Gain

*B*ecause she was writing constantly in order to finish *The Egg and I*, Betty's life suddenly became congested. Besides the writing, she was deluged with invitations to address numerous women's clubs. "Women, who formerly scarcely knew I existed, have become my best friends and insist that I come and talk to their clubs," Betty told me.

I knew how busy she was, even though she had quit her regular job to spend time on the book, but finally came an evening when she, Don, and Sydney were able to come and have dinner with my family. Betty had never made clothes a priority — "Just give me a nice raincoat, some sweaters, pants, and a couple of skirts, and I'm all set," she often said. On that particular evening, however, she wore a soft, black, sheer wool dress, trimmed in leopard fur. The colors went perfectly with her reddish-brown hair and gold-toned complexion. I complimented her and she answered, "Here I am on the threshold of fame, so Mary insisted that I buy a new dress. She had to loan me the money, though, as all of mine goes to pay the telephone company because I am making so many long-distance calls to my agent." Having to manage on a low budget, however, was soon to cease.

Later, not only did Betty fulfill speaking engagements, but radio appearances as well. "Notoriety is getting to me," she complained. "Yesterday Don and I were driving by Frederick and Nelson's and I had him stop the car while I ran in to pick up a pair of stockings. I was not dressed up, but I needed the hose for another occasion. In that short space of time I heard a woman say to her companion, 'There is Betty MacDonald. Look at the awful clothes she has on.' My privacy is out the window."

I didn't see much of Betty at that time, but I read a lot about her in the papers. Eventually, she bought a town house on the east side of Lake Union in Seattle. With the help of an architect, Betty remodeled an old house into something compact, livable, and gracious. Situated on a hillside, her new dwelling was close to the city center and had an expansive view of the lake with all its boats and the Olympic Mountains beyond. With all her commitments, she needed a Seattle base as commuting from Vashon was becoming extremely strenuous.

In September 1946, Betty was honored by Governor Mon C. Wallgren at a luncheon given at the Washington Athletic Club. He presented her with a special copy of *The Egg and I*, bound in leather. The cover was designed by a California artist and depicted a Buff Orphington setting hen.

Attending the party were Seattle's Mayor William S. Devin, who said he was reveling in Betty's reflected glory, and Bertram Lippincott, her publisher, who flew out from Philadelphia for the big event. Many newsreel men were present and sister Mary announced to them that the coming film would star Claudette Colbert and Fred MacMurray, and that Betty's daughters, Anne and Joan, would not be in the picture. Mary, who was called by one pundit, "Betty's Boswell," also announced that that was absolutely Betty's last public appearance, as she had two books to finish right away.

Betty needed some extrinsic motivation. She enjoyed relaxing with her family and many times would have to tear herself away and "chain herself," as she put it, to the typewriter. I was with her once when she was not writing, but instead, having some fun with her grandchildren and showing them off to me.

The phone rang. It was her agent, asking her if she were writing that very minute, as they were expecting certain chapters for *Onions in the Stew*. When Betty told her what she was doing, the agent asked, "Betty, do you want to be a one-book author and spend the rest of your life over a sink and ironing board, or do you want to be known for other works as well?" Betty got the message, and so did I. I left.

Often Betty shared her fan mail with me. She drew quite a contrast between the very proper, stiff letters with no pizzazz, and the ones written on a scratch tablet, perhaps a little smudged, but with sincere, warm expressions of love for her book. "These are the ones I cherish," she said.

During that period of writing *Onions in the Stew, The Plague and I,* and the *Mrs. Piggle Wiggle* stories, Betty was also involved in selling their two properties in Seattle and Vashon and buying a huge ranch in Carmel. I was in the throes of welcoming Jock home from the war, selling part of our Vashon Island property, and returning to Portland. Over an interval of about eight years, Betty and I sent each other Christmas cards — she always designed and made her own — and one or two letters per year. I happened to save a few of her letters to me and the following are some excerpts from one written in January 1956:

> I certainly thought of you all day yesterday — my how you will love Loli — one reason I love her so much is because she reminds me of you. In fact is a German Blanchie — has more friends than anyone in the whole world except you, loathes housework except for cooking, adores all animals, and is always ready to pick up and go anywhere. Yesterday in the Monterey Herald there was an ad for pets for adoption. In the ad was listed an English shepherd which is what Don wants for a cattle dog. I called the woman who runs

the agency and she acts just like you are trying to adopt a baby — demands to see your house, asks about your income, husband, children, habits — everything. Anyway the shepherd was gone, but she told me she had a black male, standard poodle less than two years old that some army officer had brought over from France and couldn't keep in Fort Ord. At first she wasn't going to let me have him because I have a female poodle and she doesn't believe in puppies — says the Peninsula is overcrowded with dogs and whenever she gives away a bitch she makes the people sign a pledge that they won't have her bred. I told her that we had 2000 acres all fenced and I was going to have Mandy bred whether she liked it or not. Then she started to investigate the people I was going to give the puppies to. I didn't dare tell her that you taught school, or she wouldn't let you have a puppy. If I do have Mandy bred, the puppies will be along in late May and will be ready by June. I hope you still want one.

I've also hired a Russian who speaks no English to help Don build some bookcases — this man used to teach in the language school and was let out with about fifty others just before Christmas. They are White Russians. Suddenly, it was decided to cut down the size of the language school and let them all go. Alex is a graduate civil engineer, and actually speaks English but with such a strong Russian accent, it is impossible to understand him. He has a good sense of humor and doesn't mind using sign language, but Don gets mad when he can't understand him and talks in a big loud bossy voice — to get even with him I've been playing a lot of Rachmaninoff records and fixing Alex big hot lunches. He has made quite a few mistakes in the bookcases, but what can you expect when Don can't speak Russian and Alex can't speak English.

There is nothing I would love more than to have you visit me and I really have some dandy people to introduce you to.

And from a July 1956 letter:

Don and I have been going to a lot of millionaire Republican parties lately and ugh, how they bore me. The last one was a picnic at an attorney's home. He is a big, fat, no-sense-of-humor, terribly successful attorney. His wife is small and brown and grasping with tiny little darting eyes and uses many little dirty expressions. There is lots of what we in our family call "peepee talk" among them all with cheap laughter and corny remarks.

We also went to a cocktail party for about 150 old admirals, generals and retired men. I haven't had my behind stroked or pinched so much in years and there is plenty to stroke and pinch too. I have been intending to go on a starvation diet, but keep testing out new recipes like chicken dipped in sour cream and fried lobster boiled in anise seed and served with onion and caviar, mayonnaise etc.

After I have been to a lot of these parties I can hardly wait to get back up here to our little cozy ranch house, and my easy, sloppy, bright Democratic friends.

Did I tell you that Mother had two very severe heart attacks? The last one when Joan and Jerry were here on their vacation. The doctor said that she couldn't possibly live through the night, but if by some miracle she did she would undoubtedly live for twenty years. She is feeling remarkably well, but can't do anything, and being idle drives her insane. But she is a very good sport about it as you would expect.

Sydney died a few months after I received this letter. Betty phoned to tell me. She said that she and Don had gone to the hospital to see Sydney in early evening. She was feeling quite well and they had a wonderful visit. On their way home, they stopped at a lookout that gave them an unobstructed view of a gorgeous sunset. They watched the sun slowly disappear, sliding smoothly down the horizon. Betty said, "It was a spiritual experience and we both felt it. We didn't speak a word the rest of the way home. Just as we entered the house, the hospital called to say that Mother had died a few minutes before. Don and I agreed that it was at the same time we had watched the spectacular sunset."

Betty felt as good as one could expect at the parting. She had never used the word *spiritual* to me before, and over the telephone, her voice reflected the reverence of her feeling.

PART

4

CHAPTER 23

Divorce and Death

After the war was over, our family moved back to Portland where Jock took another insurance job and I returned to teaching. Jock really didn't want me to teach as he thought it reflected upon his ability to support his family. I had enjoyed running the family budget while he was gone and and had accumulated a little bank account, a first for us.

Our savings soon disappeared when we re-established ourselves in Portland Heights, a very posh area not far from the city proper. In fact, the area was so high-class that at the high school Jill attended, anything fancy or expensive received the adjective "heightsy."

I had found out a number of things about myself in those last few years and felt quite independent. Little folderol expenditures bothered me, while Jock wasn't happy unless we made them. Once again we were soon enmeshed in the syndrome of keeping up appearances in the neighborhood and with friends. Appearances had top priority with Jock.

An insignificant incident happened to a family in our circle which epitomized the shallow social whirl in which we found ourselves. It had to do with high-school kids, but it reflected the level of the adult emphasis. In the Portland high schools at that time there were many social clubs or sororities with funny names like *Jama Jama* and *Wicki*. Girls from several high schools were members of these clubs, and in order to be included in them, you had to be invited. Jill joined some of them, but we did not pay much attention as we were so embroiled in solving our own problems. As long as her grades were all right, we gave her almost free rein.

Jock had a business associate whose daughter, a sweet, quiet, little girl, was not being invited to join any of the high-school clubs. Jock told me that Ray brought this problem to the office and discussed it freely. He said Ray and his wife were quite upset because Rachel was feeling very left out. They couldn't understand why she hadn't been invited as they had always been socially accepted in all the better circles.

At last one morning Ray came to the office overjoyed — Rachel had received an invitation to a tea to be given at an elegant home in the right neighborhood. At this affair she would be scrutinized to see if she were sorority material. Exactly what that meant was hard to define. As loving and dutiful parents, it was only natural that they would be concerned for their daughter's happiness. They bought her an expensive new dress and had the car washed and waxed, as they were to drive her to the party.

On the fatal Sunday they drove up to the mansion where the party was in progress. Ray stepped out of the car and opened the door for Rachel to alight. The car door made a loud and long *cree-eak*. Much to their horror, the welcoming committee was on the front porch. Rachel's parents felt sure that the uninvited squawk of the door would be a deterrent to her making the grade.

Jock and I talked about the undemocratic aspects of these high-school clubs but made no move against them. Our Jill was so happy going to her various meetings, and only involved us when she needed transportation. The Rachel episode was an eye-opener and set me thinking: values had gone awry.

But our fingers were crossed along with Rachel's and her family's, hoping she would receive the bid to join. After three days of sitting on a precarious precipice, Rachel did receive the magic bid. Ray's concern had been felt by the whole office, so he celebrated by bringing fresh doughnuts and coffee for the entire staff. This struggle for acceptance didn't phase Jock at all the way it did me. He just shrugged and said, "That's the way it goes."

For me, this high-school sorority issue was a perfect example of the social race we were in. Our present environment was constantly asking us to prove that we were "heightsy." I knew there were Portland people whose values were similar to mine, but I was not meeting them. On Vashon Island, I had not run into anything comparable to this. There were all kinds of people with all kinds of lifestyles living on one little island, and that was part of its charm.

I ruminated over my marriage to Jock. I was not happy nor was he. It occurred to me that the very so-called glamorous qualities that had attracted me to him in 1932 were causing big problems in 1951. Even though we thought we were making a supreme effort to save our marriage, we were divorced in 1952.

In later years as I evaluated that failed marriage, it came to me. Had we not two wonderful children as a result of our union, and did we not have glamorous times together? If I had continued as a "Miss Ida Greathouse" in a snow-white shirt-waist and billowy serge skirt, hovering over kids with reading problems, I would have only sterile memories. Long ago, I decided to substitute the word *fruitful* for *failed*. And I have often wanted to say, "Thank you, Mary and Betty, for your help in my having experienced that fruitful marriage."

The year 1952 was not an easy one for any of us. In the middle of this adjustment period, I received a telegram from the Seattle School District offering me a job teaching the first grade. Plans began to go forward to make the move again. Our families were up there, and many old friends with whom I had kept in touch. At last I began to appreciate all the unshowy values my family represented. Their support would help now.

Friends of ours, Flavia and Alex McEachern, with whom we had a close association in Portland, had also moved back to Seattle and were very supportive in getting the three of us settled. Once again, Betty was a major force in our lives as six years earlier it was she who had arranged for us to meet the McEacherns in the first place. At that time Flavia and I were both pregnant and became close friends immediately. Our Keith was born in June, and Flavia's boy, Scotty, in July. To this day, Scotty and his sisters, Elizabeth and Marsha, are our close friends.

In Seattle we were able to find a suitable little house close to both Esther's and the McEacherns'. We had not been there very long when I heard that Betty, too, had come back to Seattle. But the reason was not a happy one — she had cancer. She had returned because her brother-in-law, Dr. Jensen, would be able to provide her with first-rate medical attention.

Betty was staying with Mary when I went to see her. Mary's household was at its peak of activity as she was getting three daughters off to school. For the first time ever, I found Betty feeling sorry for herself. She had a good reason. Her happy life in Carmel was suddenly wrenched from her because of this dreadful disease. Even way back when she was going through her divorce from Bob, she was able to present a funny side of it, but there was no laughing now.

As I stepped into the room, she said, "I am a big *saddo*. They are all so busy I sometimes wonder if they even know I am here." We chatted awhile and tried to be *old be-happies*. I couldn't stay long because of my school duties and I went away feeling depressed.

About two weeks later on a Sunday afternoon, I was sitting out on the lawn in a deck chair, basking in an unusually hot, mid-October sun, when the phone rang. I rushed into the house to answer it before the caller hung up. It was Betty! "I am in the Maynard Hospital, and I would like a bologna sandwich with lots of mustard."

"Coming right up," I said confidently, as quite by chance I had the ingredients for just that sandwich. In less than thirty minutes I was there, handing Betty the sandwich plus a fat dill pickle. She was most pleased and seemed in fine fettle. A nurse came in, and I was scared that the bologna sandwich might be off-limits, but Betty told her about it and openly relished it.

"I came to tell you, Betty," said the nurse, "that there is a couple downstairs from Chile. They are on an extended trip around the world and one of the conditions of the trip was that the lady could find you and have a visit. She has gone to a lot of trouble tracking you down. Is it all right for them to come up?"

"Certainly," said Betty. "I would love to meet them."

Soon the lady appeared alone, saying her husband would wait downstairs. She was a lovely, dark-haired woman who spoke English quite clearly. She was all smiles, obviously thrilled that she had at last found Betty, one of her favorite authors. Betty introduced me as her best friend, and I was flattered because Betty had many friends. The woman took Betty's hand and proceeded to tell her that she had read all of her books, loved them, but related especially to the part in *Onions in the Stew* where Betty tells about having wonderful times at her own dinner parties until the guests all left or went to bed, leaving her alone in the kitchen with stacks of dirty dishes, pots, and pans. No automatic dishwashers then!

Betty's visitor said, "We have a big ranch in Chile and when people come to visit, they usually stay several days. Many times I've been left late at night with that same situation." They agreed that it was, indeed, anticlimactic to a joyful evening. The woman didn't stay long, but before she left, she wrote down Betty's address and then asked for mine as well. The meeting was both joyful and touching. I felt fortunate to have been there when one of Betty's fans had found her. All too soon, it was time for me to go, also. After giving Betty a hug, I said, "Anytime you want another sandwich, just call."

Weeks later a Christmas card arrived, identifying the signer as the woman from Chile whom I had met at Betty's bedside. Immediately, I went to the phone and called Betty, telling her of the card. "Did you get one from her, too?"

Betty didn't sound as alert and sparkly as she always had. It was obvious that she was under sedation. She said dreamily, "Blanchie, shame on you. Here I am on my deathbed, and you are out there stealing my friends!" We both laughed and said, "Good-bye." I was unaware at the time that that was to be our last talk.

A week after that, on February 7, 1958, Betty died. She would have been fifty in March. A few days later I went to a symphony concert and in the elevator, I saw Mary. The elevator was crowded, but we wriggled our way towards each other and gave one another a big hug. No words were necessary. We had lost a pal.

Now, when I think back to that last conversation over the phone, I can't help but smile. That Betty — still teasing me like always. What a great last memory!

CHAPTER *24*

The Human Comedy

*O*ne of Betty's fans once said, "Betty MacDonald wrote with a crisp candor. Her unique way with words about the most commonplace happenings left an indelible impression." The many conversations I had with Betty both amazed and amused me because of her verbal quickness in reacting to simple daily scenes. Her memory for small detail gave the commonplace a dimension of importance.

In *The Plague and I,* Betty talks about liking people:

> I like people but not all people. I'm neither Christian nor charitable enough to like anybody just because he or she is alive and breathing. I want people to interest or amuse me. I want them fascinating and witty, or so dull as to be different. I want them either intellectually stimulating or wonderfully corny; perfectly charming or one hundred percent stinker. I like my chosen companions to be distinguishable from the undulating masses, and I don't care how.

Betty listed the people who rode the early morning streetcar with her. They were the Sighers, the Silent Haters, the Big Saddos, the Non-Sleepers, and the Pretend-to-be-Cheerfuls, Laughing Boy, and Granite Eyes. I never considered her judgements to be put-downs; she was merely enjoying their differences.

Betty always made me feel important. No matter how

Betty with Sydney's dog Tudor. One of a series of pictures Betty gave the author.

much time elapsed between our visits, she would always remember my stories. Suddenly she would say, "And how is poor little 'Patched Coat'?" I had once told her about an acquaintance who bragged to everyone about this terrific man she was dating; he was taking her to fabulous places. It developed that a girl who worked in his office heard her stories and said, "What a pity she is impressed. His wife comes to the office wearing a shabby, old, patched coat!" I was most surprised when Betty remembered the tale.

One of the teachers with whom I worked met a new man. Later she confided to me, "I hope he asks me to marry him. We have so much in common. Why, just the other day we discovered that we both like our bathroom towels folded in thirds before hanging them on the rack."

Sometime later Betty said, "Say, Blanche, did those towel-folders ever marry, and how are they getting along? I suppose if they have a quarrel, they can patch it up by folding towels in thirds." Calling these people to mind out of the blue really impressed me. Betty would have been glad to know that the towel folders did marry and are still together, no doubt because of their common hobby.

Another teacher always walked into the teachers' meeting with little mincing steps, seated herself in direct line with the handsome principal, crossed her legs, and pointed her toes daintily. She arranged to have her skirt far above her knees (this was in pre-miniskirt days). I didn't really blame her for showing her legs as they were far prettier than her face. But because she was so consistent and obvious about it at every meeting, sometimes I would say, "Dixie, your skirt is way up." Whereupon she would pull it down a quarter-inch and say, "Thanks, Blanche." This answer was standard. Later, Betty would surprise me by saying, "Is 'Thanks, Blanche' still riding her skirts high?"

(When I met Betty's youngest sister, Alison, forty years later and she read this story, she exclaimed, "So that's where that expression came from. We have said 'Thanks Blanche' many times in our family, and until now I didn't know its origin.")

Betty told me about a co-worker who was trying to get her boyfriend to marry her. She used many ploys. (Unfortunately these two people did not know about the enchantment of towels folded in thirds.) Once, at a party they were sitting on a sofa, doing a little light lovemaking and gazing into a few glowing embers in the fireplace.

Betty came into the room from the back, just in time to hear the woman say as she tucked her chin on his shoulder,

"Oh, Reg, I can see into our future — three stalwart sons at our dinner table and a large Dalmation at your feet." From then on, Betty kept me posted as to the romance of "Three Stalwart Sons."

Betty, Mother and I were having a coke together in our Vashon kitchen when our neighbor, Mrs. Taylor, burst into the room all out of breath. Our houses were separated by a vacant lot which had a short uphill path, so that whenever she arrived, she was short of breath. She was a hard worker who kept her old house on the beach looking like a polished agate. Her little visits were mostly to blow off steam. As she tried to catch her breath, she would gripe about her Madrona trees always shedding leaves that had to be swept up, and all the sheets she had to change because of uninvited relatives who dropped in unexpectedly.

This particular day I saw her coming and said to Mother, "Here comes Mrs. Taylor. I wonder if she is Kem-Toning the kitchen today. (Kem-Tone was a paint applied by roller.)

Mother answered, "She probably is because yesterday she wasn't — too much work to put into a rented house."

After introducing Betty, Mrs. Taylor turned to her and asked, "Betty, what do you think I should do? I am renting this house and the kitchen has very high ceilings. They are all smoked-up and look terrible. I don't know whether to Kem-Tone or not."

"If the smoked-up ceiling is making you unhappy and you have the energy, maybe you should Kem-Tone," Betty said.

The next day Mrs. Taylor came back. "Tell your friend Betty that I took her advice and did *not* Kem-Tone. The smoke is not making me that unhappy and I sure didn't have the energy like she said."

Months later when I saw Betty, the first thing she asked was if Mrs. Taylor had ever Kem-Toned her kitchen. Betty was interested to hear that Mrs. Taylor finally did Kem-Tone because more relatives were coming and that was all the motivation she needed to do the job.

All of this was minutiae in the scheme of living, but Betty thrived on observing people and their foibles. So did I. We both loved people. From the first moments of our friendship at Lincoln High School in front of our lockers to the very last times we talked together, it was the ordinariness of everyday living that drew us close. Betty drained to the dregs the full cup of human comedy.

Epilogue

by ALISON BARD BURNETT

$\mathcal{B}$lanche Caffiere has written this wonderful story of her friendship with my sister, Betty. It is a delightful and true story. As Betty's youngest sister, my relationship with her was special. When we were children, our interests were very different, but later, when I married and had a family of my own, we lived near each other and became close friends.

It was my good fortune to be in on Betty's fabulous success when she wrote her best seller. In fact, I happened to be with her at the rural mailbox when the first check for ten thousand dollars arrived from the publisher.

We immediately went to Kimmel's, the Vashon Island grocery store, to buy food for a celebration dinner. Eating good food was the way our family honored an event. We paid no attention to prices, but chose goodies in abandon. The most impressive article was the wild rice — three bags at $2.50 each. We also bought the best wine the store had to offer and a beautiful, fresh king salmon.

I had always budgeted my grocery money, but not that day. When the purchases were added up, the bill came to more than I spent on food in a month. But the dinner was one to remember!

Betty's daughters, Ann and Joan, spent the dinner hour making lists of clothes to buy, outfits they had always longed for. Betty was never one to spend money on herself but she loved to give presents. Each member of the family received an exquisite gift, and she extended her generosity even further, giving her cleaning lady and husband a trip to Norway to see their parents who had been hiding in the mountains during the war. Mrs. Hanson was overwhelmed with gratitude as her parents died shortly after the visit.

Betty enjoyed my children along with me. When my older son, Darsie, was born he was the first boy in our family, Betty adored him, and he loved her. Betty and I laughed over the things they did and said; together we read their fascinating books to them, and my daughter, Alison, owes her very life to the timely advice Betty gave me when Alison was a tiny baby.

When Betty's checks began coming in regularly, she was amused at her own affluence, the way money was rolling in — and rolling out just as fast. Once when my two-year-old son, Bard, was visiting her, he wanted a piece of paper on which to draw a truck. Since none was provided immediately, he foraged for himself. Soon he handed Betty his finished creation on a small slip of paper. She howled with laughter, while Bard looked a bit hurt. Betty hugged him close. "Bardo, now we know you're one of us." He had drawn his truck on the back of a check made out for eight thousand dollars.

About the Author

*B*lanche Caffiere graduated from Western Washington University and holds a Masters degree from Lewis and Clark College in Portland. She has taught school in Washington, Oregon and Africa, as well as London, England as a Fulbright exchange teacher.

The author's previous publications include contributions to two histories of Vashon Island, Washington, *Past Remembered I* and *Past Remembered II*; *Ferry Tales*, a book about Puget Sound ferryboats; and numerous articles on education in the *Christian Science Monitor* and other publications.

Blanche Caffiere makes her home on Vashon Island with her husband, where she takes tap-dancing lessons and knits. *Much Laughter, A Few Tears* is her first full-length work, published at the age of eighty-five.